Struggling for Survival

Development, Conflict, and Social Change Series

Series Editors
Scott Whiteford and William Derman
Michigan State University

Struggling for Survival: Workers, Women, and Class on a Nicaraguan State Farm, Gary Ruchwarger

Deep Water: Development and Change in Pacific Village Fisheries, Margaret Critchlow Rodman

Kilowatts and Crisis: Hydroelectric Power and Social Dislocation in Eastern Panama, Alaka Wali

The Spiral Road: Change in a Chinese Village Through the Eyes of a Communist Party Leader, Huang Shu-min

Ancestral Rainforests and the Mountain of Gold: Political Ecology of the Wopkaimin People of Central New Guinea, David Hyndman

Agrarian Reform in El Salvador, Martin Diskin

Surviving Drought and Development: The Ariaal of Northern Kenya, Elliot M. Fratkin

Struggling for Survival

Workers, Women, and Class on a Nicaraguan State Farm

Gary Ruchwarger

Westview Press
BOULDER, SAN FRANCISCO, & LONDON

Development, Conflict, and Social Change Series

Photos by Todd Alwine and Kim Powick; reprinted by permission

Published in 1989 in the United States of America by Westview Press, Inc., 5500 Central Avenue, Boulder, Colorado 80301, and in the United Kingdom by Westview Press, 13 Brunswick Centre, London WC1N 1AF, England

Library of Congress Cataloging-in-Publication Data
Ruchwarger, Gary.
  Struggling for survival: workers, women, and class on a
Nicaraguan state farm / Gary Ruchwarger.
     p. cm.—(Development, conflict, and social change series)
  Includes bibliographical references.
  ISBN 0-8133-7407-3
  1. State farms—Nicaragua—Case studies.   2. Agricultural
laborers—Nicaragua—Case studies.   3. Women in agriculture—
Nicaragua—Case studies.   4. Social classes—Nicaragua—Case
studies.   I. Title.   II. Series.
HD1493.N5R83   1989
306.3′49—dc20
                                                    89-37521
                                                         CIP

138058

Contents

Illustrations

Preface

Despite the plethora of works on the Nicaraguan revolution, no book examines the workings of a state enterprise. I therefore approached this study with the goal of providing an analysis of some key aspects of class and gender relations on a Nicaraguan state farm. To gather direct knowledge of these relations, I conducted 14 months of primary research on the Oscar Turcios Chavarria enterprise just outside the town of Estelí. I spent much of the period from December 1986 to September 1988 interviewing company employees, attending union and management meetings, and studying enterprise documents.

I am indebted to Hector Valdivia, the state farm's director, who granted me complete access to enterprise reports and a wide-ranging interview at the conclusion of my research. Special thanks must also go to Vivian Peres and Julian Salinas, the two men who sucessively held the post of general secretary of the enterprise union during the 1986–1988 period. Both union leaders provided me with frequent interviews and shared dozens of documents with me. I am also grateful to Alberto Martinez, the regional secretary of organization in the Rural Workers Association, who was always ready to answer my many queries concerning union policies. Among the other union officials who provided me with unusual opportunities to observe rank-and-file union activities were Melania Castillo and Nohelia Gutierrez. I also wish to thank Marietta Paz, the state farm's personnel director, for her patient replies to my questions about the frequent changes in the enterprise's wage and incentive system.

I am particularly grateful to Suzanne Lebell who, during the last three months of work, assisted me immensely in research, word processing, and editorial tasks. She conducted this work under trying conditions that included uninterrupted rainfall, amoeba attacks, insect invasions, and my sporadic intemperance. Finally, thanks are due to Blanca and Mercedes Arroliga for their painstaking collection of data on worker productivity and wages.

Gary Ruchwarger
March 1989

Introduction

Now in its tenth year the Nicaraguan revolution has been studied from many perspectives. But few writers have attempted to analyze the revolution's drive to transform the country's relations of production. By offering a case study of a Nicaraguan state farm, this book aims to contribute to such an analysis. In focusing on class and gender, it reveals some aspects of the revolution's evolving production relations. I say *some* aspects because, from the view of Marxist theory, any society's relations of production—or any other set of social relations—are tremendous collections of diverse processes, activities, and relationships interconnected in complex contradictions. To fully analyze them all in a systematic presentation would take vast numbers of Marxist theorists immense amounts of time. Writing in their seminal study, *Knowledge and Class*, Stephen A. Resnick and Richard D. Wolff depict this dilemma with uncommon frankness:

> From the Marxian standpoint, the task of a comprehensive social analysis is in principle not achievable, neither for Marxian nor for any other kind of theory. It is rather like human beings achieving birdlike flight or avoiding death or eliminating all loneliness from a lifetime. Like those impossibilities, the human incapacity to produce complete social analyses need not and should not bother us very much. To deny or dwell morosely upon our limitations promises little beyond bitter disappointment or bouts of depression or both. The point is rather to recognize the limitations that influence but do not prevent our efforts to build productive personal and social situations.[1]

In this spirit, then, I offer a partial analysis of some of the social processes underway on a Nicaraguan state farm. But before analyzing the enterprise's class and gender relations, I will devote this introduction to a discussion of the key themes explored by this book.

Why Class Analysis?

A class analysis of revolutionary Nicaragua's state sector is important for two fundamental reasons. First, the Sandinistas are determined to overhaul Nicaragua's socioeconomic structure, ending the "exploitation of man by man [sic]." But is it possible to abolish exploitation through nationalizing productive resources? Can a revolutionary society with a poorly educated working class avoid creating a new managerial class—an elite of administrators and technicians that run the state sector in the name of workers and peasants? An analysis of wage policies and struggles among state farm employees over incentives, reclassifications, and the piece-rate system provides some answers to these questions.

Second, a class analysis of a state-run agricultural enterprise reveals the contradictions created by export agriculture. As I detail in chapter one, the Oscar Turcios Chavarria state farm earns 90 percent of its income from the export of tobacco. An increasingly important earner of foreign exchange for Nicaragua, tobacco requires substantial inputs, the intensive use of manual labor, and a well-trained staff of agronomists to oversee quality control. The demands of export agriculture thus engender production relations that tend to contradict specific goals of the revolution. How do the organizations that mediate class relations on state farms resolve conflicts between workers inspired by the "popular power" slogans of the revolution and an administrative stratum determined to earn dollars for an economy desperately in need of foreign exchange? Only an examination of class structure within a state enterprise can uncover the problems raised by these contradictory interests.

The State Farm's Class Structure

My research at the Oscar Turcios Chavarria state farm indicates that three distinct social classes are emerging in Nicaragua's state sector: a working class, a coordinator class, and a managerial class. In defining the working class I follow Marx's conception in which workers include those people who are "owners merely of labor power." In defining the managerial and coordinator classes I draw on the recent work of scholars who are attempting to apply Marxist theory to postcapitalist social formations.[2] For, although the Nicaraguan social formation is not socialist, its state sector possesses many of the characteristics of "actually existing socialism."

Following the recent writing of Resnick and Wolff, I hold that Marx's concept of class differentiates people not according to the "productive assets" that they possess or lack, but according to their participation in the production or extraction of surplus labor. One social formation differs from another, Marx asserts in *Capital* 3.42, according to the "specific form in which unpaid surplus labor is pumped out of the direct producers."[3] It is the mechanism of exploitation that determines the relationship of rulers and ruled. This mechanism emerges directly out of production and reacts upon it—a relationship corresponding to a definite stage in the development of technology and the capacity of labor to produce a surplus. And it is this relationship that in turn "reveals the innermost secret, the hidden basis of the entire social structure, and with it the political form of the relation of sovereignty and dependence, in short, the corresponding specific form of the state."[4]

In Nicaragua's state sector, workers, or "direct producers," perform necessary and surplus labor, while managers extract or appropriate surplus labor. But Nicaraguan managers do not appropriate surplus labor directly in the form of receiving surplus value as do productive capitalists in the capitalist fundamental class process. Rather, as Donald C. Hodges contends, managers in Nicaragua's state sector appropriate workers' surplus labor *indirectly*, in the form of relatively high salaries.

> The source of surplus value under socialism is not "variable capital"— the capacity of labor power to produce a value greater than its own value— but the assignment of a value to labor services that is less than what they produce. Unlike the capitalist mechanism of exploitation based on the commodity labor power and the operation of market forces, the socialist mechanism is based on an economic plan in which services are assessed according to a hierarchy of ranks within the limits imposed by a fixed budget. The capitalist pumps out a surplus by paying for the full value of labor power; the bureaucrat sucks it out by *not paying* labor services their full value. In each case a different type of exploitation is the source of a different kind of privilege: profits under capitalism, salaries under socialism.[5]

Borrowing from the work of Erik Olin Wright and Hodges, I also contend that an intermediate class is forming in Nicaragua. I call the members of this class "coordinators," experts whose control of skills and knowledge within production allow them to appropriate some of the surplus out of production. Agreeing with Hodges, I believe this class can be distinguished clearly from both the managerial and working classes:

> Unlike a great exploiting class, a class of petty exploiters has an upper as well as a lower limit to its sharing in surplus value. Within the framework of Marx's labor theory of value, let us suppose x is the average wage for manual workers at a rate of exploitation of 100 percent. During an eight-hour day a manual worker produces a commodity worth x in four hours,

but he works another four hours to produce a second x for the exploiters. Then $2x$ will be the lower limit separating the intermediate class of petty exploiters from the workers below, and $4x$ will be the upper limit separating it from the exploiting class above. Here we have the economic basis for distinguishing between a petty-bureaucratic and a bureaucratic class.[6]

It is noteworthy that Nicaragua's National System of Ordering Work and Salaries (SNOTS), which establishes a hierarchy of ranks within a global wage and salary system, places technical and professional employees in a separate wage category in which they earn between two and four times the average wage of a Nicaraguan worker. In chapter two I define these employees in terms of their "skill assets," and outline their position in the state farm's class structure. Most coordinators in Nicaragua are organized in the Sandinista-affiliated Confederation of Professionals, an organization that has been pressing recently for higher salaries and more decision-making powers for its members.

Before concluding this section on class, it must be emphasized that the three groups I distinguish in Nicaragua's state sector are *classes in formation*. Developing in a revolutionary process only a decade old, these collectivities are forming as a result of economic struggles. Economic struggles, however, always appear historically in their concrete articulation within the totality of struggles, always in a form molded by political and ideological relations.[7] In chapter two I will describe the effects that wage struggles have on the process of class formation in a particular enterprise, revealing the complexity of class organization in Nicaragua's state sector.

But class relations are not the only set of relations undergoing transformation in the Sandinista revolution; gender relations are also undergoing fundamental change. I now turn to a discussion of these relations.

Why Gender Relations?

There are two reasons for my emphasis on gender relations on the state farm.[8] First, women comprise 60 percent of the permanent workers on the enterprise and 75 percent of all temporary workers. To ignore sexual politics in examining any enterprise in which women work is sexist; to ignore gender relations in studying a work center with such a large percentage of women would be absurd. Second, the Sandinistas insist that women's liberation is fundamental to their revolutionary project. A case study of a Nicaraguan state enterprise must analyze the extent to which gender relations are being transformed within the context of the revolution's restructuring of production relations.

Gender Inequality in Nicaragua

In this book it will be argued that women's family roles cannot be ignored in an analysis of gender relations on the state farm. Gender inequality faced by women wage workers in Nicaragua involves not only subordination in the work place, as low-paid members of the working class, but also oppression in the home, resulting from a strongly patriarchal family structure.

Although the revolution has improved women's political economic condition, and has brought some changes in the relations between men and women as well, these changes certainly have not spelled an end to patrariachy. About half of Nicaraguan women are employed, a very high percentage for a Latin American country. But while wage work outside the home may bring a woman more independence and freedom, it has also created a dual burden for most women, who are still held responsible for the care of home and children. Several studies indicate that this dual burden may lead to severe stress and alienation, particularly among working-class women, who cannot afford to hire domestic help.[9] Thus, even when women work, they are *incompletely proletarianized.* They tend to view their family roles as primary, and to see their jobs as another way of aiding their families.

Indeed, the family is the core of Nicaraguan society. It serves as social network, support system, and unit for child-rearing. Women play the central role in the Nicaraguan family—a role that can inhibit their ability to be workers, activists, and soldiers, but which makes them essential in other ways. Women maintain the labor force, raise children, clean up neighborhoods, and care for the sick. Women serve as unpaid social workers, thereby aiding a country too poor to pay for many such public social services.

Most Nicaraguan women experience the family as something unstable and changeable, quite different from the durable nuclear model. Few women get married, but nearly all begin bearing children between the ages of 15 and 19. Women head 40 percent of the families in the country, rearing their children without a male partner.[10] Because a large percentage of women have to work outside the home, relatives often take charge of the children. In many cases, though, children are left to take care of themselves.

Although women play the dominant role in the upbringing of their children, men wield tremendous power within the family, controlling the household finances. Even families with an absent father can feel his presence. For instance, the mother tends to speak favorably of the father to her children and often portrays herself as "helpless" without him, thereby reinforcing sexist family stereotypes. A group of English feminists, who interviewed scores of Nicaraguan women in 1982, describe the ways in which sexism permeates the Nicaraguan family.

> *Machismo*, which is deeply ingrained in Nicaraguan men, underlies relations between them and their families. A display of male superiority, one of its characteristics is the assumption of male privilege and power in the family: the man is "master" of his "own" woman—to the point even of physical violence. Women are defined essentially in terms of their reproductive functions and as mothers are expected to bear the practical responsibility for bringing up a family. The cult of virility dictates that a rigid division of sexual roles must be maintained and housework is left entirely to women. Though men often expect their women to bear many children, quite often they simply abandon their families, often described as "irresponsible paternity."[11]

The extended family provides Nicaraguan women with a crucial support system. Most homes comprise parents and children as well as grandparents, aunts, uncles, and other relatives. As an interdependent unit, the extended family furnishes women with both economic and emotional sustenance. A woman's relations with her sisters, brothers, and mother are often more important than those with her male partner.

Yet the Nicaraguan family is subject to substantial pressures. In the countryside, most men who journey to other jobs during the year maintain relations with a second or third woman in the area of their seasonal work, and frequently they have children with these women. Many men in urban areas also have relationships and children with more than one woman. The lack of privacy in town and city dwellings can strain family relations. In the poor neighborhoods of Managua, 65 percent of the houses have only one bedroom, in which as many as six or seven family members sleep.[12] This often contributes to spousal conflicts, jealousy, alcoholism, fatigue, and promiscuity.

However, the dual burden borne by women workers at the Oscar Turcios state farm does not go unchallenged. As we will see, rural women workers in Nicaragua are waging a difficult struggle to overcome their subordination in the home as well as in the workplace.

Notes

1. Richard D. Wolff and Stephen A. Resnick, *Economics: Marxian versus Neoclassical* (Baltimore/London: The Johns Hopkins University Press, 1987), p. 141.

2. See the appendix for a detailed discussion of recent Marxist theories of the class structure of postcapitalist societies.

3. Quoted in Hodges, *The Bureaucratization of Socialism*, p. 62.

4. Quoted in ibid., p. 62.

5. Ibid., p. 75.

6. Ibid., p. 46.

7. Adam Przeworski, "Proletariat into a Class: The Process of Class Formation from Karl Kautsky's *The Class Struggle* to Recent Controversies," *Politics and Society*, p. 372.

8. See the appendix for an in-depth analysis of recent feminist theories of gender inequality.

9. See, for example, Louise Lamphere, "Women's Work, Alienation and Class Consciousness," (paper presented at 72nd annual meeting of the American Anthropological Association, New Orleans, 1973) and Virve Piho, "Life and Labor of the Female Textile Worker in Mexico City," in R. Rohrlich-Leavitt (The Hague: Mouton, 1976).

10. Deighton, et al., *Sweet Ramparts: Women in Revolutionary Nicaragua* (London: War on Want and Nicaraguan Solidarity Campaign, 1983), p. 124.

11. Ibid., p. 125.

12. Instituto Historico Centroamericano, "The Nicaraguan Family in a Time of Transition," *Envio* (April 1984), p. 2c.

The State Farm and
Its Economic Context

1 This chapter begins by outlining the context in which the state farm operates, surveying the nature of Nicaragua's mixed economy, the pre-revolutionary structure of agriculture, the formation of state farms, the rural class structure, and the workings of the Rural Workers Association. We then discuss the state farm, focussing on its structure and size, its relations with state institutions, and its administrative problems. Finally, we deal with the problem of labor shortages in the agricultural sector, concentrating on the problem of low wages that plagues the entire economy. Such an overview of the state farm and its context will help clarify the workings of the state farm, and the tremendous constraints that inhibit its development. We will then be ready to examine the class relations on the state farm.

The Mixed Economy

After Somoza's overthrow the Nicaraguan people inherited a devastated economy. Somoza's looting had left only $3.5 million in the treasury, not enough to pay for two days' worth of imports. Somoza's bombers had destroyed schools, hospitals, and workplaces in Nicaragua's major towns, including several dozen factories owned by opposition industrialists. Capital flight during the civil war had also damaged the economy: $220 million in 1978 and $315 million in the first half of 1979. In Managua, more than one-third of the labor force was unemployed. Production levels had regressed to those of 1962. Because of the fighting, 70 percent of the cultivable land had not been planted, affecting both cash crops and food staples. The internal dislocation of the population fleeing the repression and the cities where there was fighting, the emigration—temporary or permanent—of many capitalists and their capital, the blockade of roads, the theft of thousands of head of cattle to Honduras, all of this severely crippled the agricultural sector leaving many Nicaraguans facing the specter of hunger.[1]

The new revolutionary government that took power on July 19, 1979, faced a formidable economic crisis. It set three major goals for the economic system: (1) to rebuild the devasted economy; (2) to redistribute income and economic influence toward the workers and peasants; and (3) to dismantle the economic base of the old regime.[2] One of the new government's first acts was the confiscation of properties and enterprises that had formerly been owned by Somoza and his collaborators.[3] The new government also nationalized the bankrupt financial system, the insurance companies, foreign trade, and the country's run-down mining sector. These confiscated properties and holdings formed the foundation for the new state sector of the economy, called the *Area de Propriedad del Pueblo* (Area of People's Property—APP). The government turned over management of the confiscated agricultural holdings to the new *Instituto Nicaragüense de Reforma Agraria* (Nicaraguan Institute of Agrarian Reform—INRA), and placed most of the manufacturing plants in the hands of the new *Corporación de Industrias del Pueblo* (Corporation of People's Industries—COIP). The revolutionary state thus assumed control over a major proportion of the means of production and took responsibility for reorganizing and reactivating the economy.

The new government, however, made no attempt to socialize the entire productive process or eliminate private capital. Rather, the government offered guarantees to the private sector that private property would be respected and that private enterprise would be encouraged to take part in the reactivation and development of the economy. Since the early days of the revolution, the political leadership has stressed that the elimination of private enterprise and an extensive socialization of the means of production have not been among their goals. According to Jaime Wheelock, Minister of Agricultural Development and Agrarian Reform,

> It is important to understand that the socialist model is a solution for contradictions that only exist in developed capitalist countries. Now, for a series of reasons, many of them political, and others having to do with hunger and desperation, certain peoples have made a revolution in the worst conditions of social development. . . . This is our case. Even though we have socialist principles, we cannot effect the transformation of our society by socializing the means of production. This would not lead to socialism, rather, on the contrary, it could lead to the destruction and disarticulation of our society.[4]

The Sandinistas, therefore, do not think it is possible to socialize all the means of production in an underdeveloped country such as Nicaragua.

Consequently, they seek the cooperation of private enterprise in the development of a "mixed economy," which includes five forms of property: state, cooperative, small private, medium private, and large private. The state sector now comprises approximately 40 percent of the gross domestic product and the three forms of private production account for the remaining 60 percent. In agriculture and manufacturing—the two main productive sectors of the economy—private producers generate an even larger proportion of total production. The place of private property in Nicaragua's mixed enonomy is therefore more significant than most outsiders realize. In fact, revolutionary Nicaragua has a smaller state sector than Peru under General Velasco's reformist military regime, or Argentina under Peron's populist regime, or even Chile under Allende's Popular Unity government.

On the other hand, capitalists are not free to set the pace for the Nicaraguan economy. The government possesses an array of powers that act to restrain and reduce subversion of the Sandinista economic program. The Central Bank regulates the allocation of credit and foreign exchange to both the private and the APP sectors. And though the various banks operate semi-independently from each other, they do so because they are specialized in different areas.[5] In addition, all Nicaraguan exports and imports are under the control of various bodies within the Ministry of Foreign Trade. The government, with its national import and export companies and its control over foreign exchange, regulates the volume and nature of investment in the entire productive sector. This, together with state administration of the credit structure, allows the government to influence the form and structure of private sector development, and to plan economic growth in terms of social need. Consequently, the revolutionary government "goes against the logic of capital accumulation without breaking it."[6]

The Sandinistas stress that their support of a mixed economy does not contradict the revolution's primary commitment to defend the interests of the country's poor majority, especially the peasants and workers. In 1983, Sandinista leader Jaime Wheelock revealed the meaning of a mixed economy in the Nicaraguan context:

> The hegemony of the economic development process is in the new relations of production created by the revolution. It is a hegemony achieved with the nationalization of foreign commerce, of natural resources and of strategic industrial sectors, and with the nationalization of the banks. With these measures we have created a system of production and of management which predominates, which is hegemonic, which coexists with forms one could call capitalist to an appreciable degree, and with others that are backward or precapitalist.

Our tendency is that state and cooperative properties will be hegemonic, coexisting with medium and small, and even large, private production, in which the backward relations of capitalism will surely become secondary, subordinated.[7]

The Pre-Revolutionary Structure of Nicaraguan Agriculture

Lacking a productive base in the large hacienda, the plantation, or the mining enclave, the structure of Nicaraguan agriculture differs markedly from the rest of Central America and Latin America. This sets the Sandinista revolution apart from the Mexican, Cuban, and Bolivian revolutionary processes. Nicaragua's agricultural sector is characterized by the important role played by the petty and medium bourgeoisie and by wage labor.

Two other key features of Nicaragua's agrarian structure are: (1) the historical absence of peonage (the use of laborers bound in servitude because of indebtedness to landowners), and (2) a small population and large areas of uncultivated land. The first of these features led to the early introduction of wage labor, while the second has generated expansionary settlements in the agricultural frontier.

Eduardo Baumeister, a student of Nicaragua's agrarian reform, summarizes the capitalist development of Nicaraguan agriculture in theoretical terms:

> We find the junker road, involving the transition from the pre-capitalist hacienda based on the use of a serf-like labour force to the use of wage labour by the large capitalist landowner engaged in cattle-raising and the cultivation of coffee. At the same time we find the formation of small and medium-sized units of production along the agricultural frontier with the capacity to proletarianize local labour or to attract it from other zones. We also find the classical form of land-leasing in the cotton-producing areas of the Pacific Coast. Finally, we find intensive agriculture in the form of capitalist plantations producing sugar cane, irrigated rice and tobacco.[8]

Pre-revolutionary agriculture was also characterized by the rapid expansion in production and the area under cultivation that occurred between the end of World War II and the early 1970s. This was due to the introduction of new products—cotton, irrigated rice, and tobacco— as well as the increased production of coffee, cattle, and sugar. This expansion in production doubled the land area under cultivation and intensified the proletarianization of the peasantry. In addition, the expulsion of small peasant producers from the land that accompanied the growth of cotton and cattle production led to a significant decline in basic grain production. This dynamic growth of agriculture during the post-World War II period—common to the rest of Central America—distinguished the Nicaraguan situation from the Cuban case, in which many years of economic stagnation (mainly in the crucial sugar sector) preceded the revolution.

Nicaragua's rural class structure prior to the revolution was dominated by two well-defined sectors. The first was the Somocista sector made up of properties owned by Somoza, his family, and close allies. Although possessing significant land holdings in sugar, rice, and tobacco, this sector was predominant in agro-industry—coffee mills, rice mills, sugar mills, slaughter houses, and cotton mills. The Somocista sector also dominated commerce and banking. The second sector of the agrarian bourgeoisie was comprised of landowners with medium and large landholdings who were primarily producers of traditional agricultural export commodities—coffee, cattle, and cotton. This sector was also involved to a lesser degree in agro-industry, commerce, and the financial sphere.

Subordinate to these two hegemonic sectors of the rural bourgeoisie was a large peasant class which largely produced basic foods such as corn, beans, and cheese. Within the family economy the peasantry reproduced the bulk of the labor force required by agroexport capitalism. Tens of thousands of men and women from peasant families toiled as temporary wage workers on cotton, coffee, tobacco, and sugar plantations during the harvest season. During the rest of the year they were confined to the worst plots of land in the country, cultivating the land with a backward technology.

Given the structural elements and production dynamics before 1979, Nicaragua did not provide the grounds for a democratic bourgeois revolution. Precapitalist elements were marginal, and commercial and financial capitalists did not inhibit the growth of productive capital. As a result, a profound structural transformation was not required to free the country from the dominance of a precapitalist hierarchy. Moreover, neither social nor political conditions warranted the development of collective forms of production as the primary form in the early revolutionary period. Most agriculture and a significant percentage of industry was owned by small and medium-sized producers, including rich peasants, small landlords with capital, and the minor bourgeoisie. Also, with no peasant community tradition on which to build, peasants could not be quickly drawn into collectivized production. Peasants who have joined cooperatives come from backgrounds similar to those of the rural proletariat.

To maintain a broad base of national unity that includes all the propertied sectors and to prevent a process of individual peasantization that would lead to a mass of small property-owners, the Nicaraguan government has departed from the classical bourgeois democratic model of agrarian reform. The main components of the Sandinista agrarian reform policy include: (1) the creation of a state sector from the holdings expropriated from the Somocistas; (2) the distribution of a portion of the expropriated properties to the workers of these lands or to the peasants who fought for the land in these zones so that they can be farmed collectively in what are known as Sandinista Agricultural Cooperatives; (3) the reduction of land rents and the onerous terms for leasing land; (4) the provision of credit to all sectors of the agricultural population; and (5) the nationalization of a part of domestic trade and all foreign trade.

Since this book focuses on a state farm, I will describe the process that led to the Sandinistas' decision to convert confiscated Somocista estates into state enterprises.

The Formation of State Farms

The transformation of Nicaragua's rural structure began before the 1979 Sandinista victory, as peasants and farmworkers seized Somocista land holdings during the war against the dictatorship. The Rural Workers Association backed these land takeovers, which mainly occurred around the Pacific Coast city of Leon during the final months of the popular insurrection. The seizures not only vindicated the economic and political struggles of the rural workers and peasants, but also provided the food necessary to inhabitants in the liberated areas. Between June and August 1979, peasants collectively farmed the seized land, refraining from converting farms into individual holdings.

The day after the dictatorship's collapse, Decree No. 3 of the National Government of Reconstruction authorized the confiscation of all the landholdings of Somoza and his allies. All at once, this decree initiated the nationalization of almost two million acres in approximately 2,000 farms and ranches. Because the bulk of these ex-Somocista farms were modern large-scale enterprises, the Sandinistas feared that productivity would drop if they were parceled up.

The production units formerly owned by the Somozas, the military and their associates were large, highly mechanized plantations into which huge investments in the millions were channeled, often from the national treasury. Breaking them up into a myriad of parcels would decrease or eliminate the possibility of employing the technology and machinery that had been put into them and, consequently, would reduce their productivity. We realized that it was absolutely necessary to keep the production units intact. Had we not [acted] immediately, the campesinos would have occupied this land themselves and would have parceled it out in the traditional way.[9]

The state, however, still had to decide whether to transfer the title to these lands to production cooperatives or retain title and manage the farms itself. The Sandinistas decided to create state farms, justifying their decision with three arguments. First, the success of these farms was crucial to guarantee the ongoing receipt of foreign exchange. Second, these highly developed properties had been run with a small permanent labor force and a large seasonal work force; worker ownership could easily generate a rural elite. If the state had direct control of the surplus created on these farms, it could distribute the benefits throughout the population. Third, the Sandinistas thought that it would be easier to generate more jobs—so desperately needed by landless farmworkers—under state administration than on worker-owned lands.

While government leaders felt that circumstances dictated developing state farms on the confiscated land, the Sandinistas nevertheless antic- ipated some positive consequences. They expected, for example, that state farms would promote worker participation in management and that the profits could be used to benefit the popular sectors in Nicaragua. The Sandinistas also believed they could avoid some of the problems that state farms have faced in other countries. Unlike the Soviet Union, where state farms were created by collectivizing small, privately owned farms, in Nicaragua the process simply entailed the conversion to public ownership of already existing large, centrally managed farms.

The government devoted the first year and a half to developing some measure of organization to the 2,000 confiscated farms. The Nicaraguan Institute of Agrarian Reform grouped the state farms in a three-tiered management system. Geographically contingent farms were organized into 1,200 production units or *Unidades de Produción* (UPEs). INRA grouped these units into 170 complexes, called *Complejos Agricolas,* organized by product. The Institute then gathered the regional complexes into twenty-seven state agricultural enterprises, known as *Empresas Agricolas.* INRA established this structure to take advantage of both centralized and decentralized forms of management.

The large state farms that included an industrial processing plant were under the responsibility of Agro-Inra, a special subdivision of INRA. Agro-Inra organized these farms by product. In 1980 Agro-Inra managed ten enterprises that included sugar, rice, tobacco, cotton, coffee, meat slaughtering and packing, hog production, food processing, and animal feed enterprises.[10]

The Rural Class Structure

Of the 500,000 Nicaraguans engaged in agriculture during the late 1970s, approximately twenty percent were landless wage workers who could find employment only four months of the year during the coffee, sugar cane, and cotton harvests. These agricultural workers were primarily victims of a period of expanded cotton production in the 1950s and 1960s, when landowners expelled tenants and sharecroppers from the haciendas; similar "land clearance" occurred in the sixties and seventies with the expansion of cattle ranches. In addition, the vast majority of peasants who possessed land did not have sufficient land to meet their subsistence needs. Consequently, they were compelled to work for the big landowners during the harvest season. In total, almost eighty percent of the rural labor force was engaged in wage labor.[11]

Orlando Nuñez, a Sandinista economist, notes that this agricultural work force was characterized by a forced mobility.

> Although the seasonally-employed agricultural proletariat might be the most numerous group during four months of the year . . . , they survive unemployed or as semiproletarians, going from the cotton, coffee, and sugar harvests on the plantations back to their peasant plots, from the countryside to the city where they struggle for survival, unemployed or underemployed.[12]

This very mobility tended to draw together some of the most oppressed sectors of the population. Deere and Marchetti note that most peasants shared the same fate as the rural workers.

> Middle peasant farmers who have sufficient access to land are organizationally isolated from one another. While they are also exploited by merchants and usurers, their exploitation is not so easily identified. In contrast, the vast sector of smallholders without sufficient access to land migrated for four months out of the year to the harvests to engage in wage work. There they lived in the most wretched conditions and worked 12 to 15 hours a day picking coffee or cotton only to be cheated out of a day's work by crooked measuring scales. For these months of the year, their conditions were one and the same with the landless rural workers and those workers either permanently employed on the haciendas or who were given access to land on the haciendas as sharecroppers or renters.[13]

Thus, the form of agroindustrial capitalism that emerged in Nicaragua produced an unequally developed proletariat, with an extraordinary occupational instability and an incompleted process of separation from the means of production. However, despite the seasonal nature of wage labor in the countryside and the unfinished process of separation from the means of production, the real size of the rural proletariat should not be underestimated. Indeed, as Carlos Vilas emphasizes, it is misleading to speak of an agricultural *subproletariat* in Nicaragua even though many rural workers sell their labor power seasonally, for lack of stable employment:

> The concept of *proletarianization of the labor force* refers to the way in which direct producers are related to the means of production and confront capital, a relation of dispossession and of opposition. Their salaried situation derives from this relation, but it is not a mechanical derivation, since it is mediated by the effective possibility each worker has to find a salaried job. Whether or not it is found, the worker's condition as a proletarian is not altered.
>
> Consequently, the seasonality of this or that activity—in this case the harvest of exportable agricultural products—determines the seasonality of work, but does not in turn make the class situation of the labor force seasonal. *What is seasonal is employment, not the class or fraction that fills this employment.* The labor force does not cease being proletarianized by the fact that its labor relation with a given capitalist ends; it continues being proletarian with respect to capital in general. Workers affected by this cyclical movement of demand for labor power and by the general level of agricultural activity have been forced to seek other occupations or to endure longer or shorter periods of unemployment, but none of this detracts from their proletarian character.[14]

Various studies carried out after the triumph of the revolution tend to confirm Vilas' view. These studies indicate that during the late 1970s the agricultural proletariat averaged between 120,000 and 130,000—approximately one-third of the agricultural EAP. Only some 50,000 had permanent waged work throughout the year, while the rest had fixed employment for only two or three months. They toiled as an *itinerant proletariat* the remainder of the year, moving from the cotton and coffee harvest to urban services, construction, or other tasks, generally maintaining their salaried conditions.[15]

This permanent proletariat is complemented by a large *semiproletariat* of poor peasants, *minifundists*, who are unable to subsist on the product of their farm, and who are forced to sell their labor power to other producers. This fraction of the rural labor force makes up two-thirds of the peasantry—some 165,000 people—and accounts for more than a third of the agricultural EAP. As Vilas notes, this is a portion of the labor force characterized by a movement toward proletarianization:

> The impoverishment of the small peasantry and the seasonality of employment in agroexports forces these workers to suffer a process of *proletarianization-deproletarianization;* said another way, this is one of the peculiar forms of the proletarianization process of the agroexport capitalist model.[16]

Clearly the economy's dependence on a few export crops has a direct impact on the working population, pressuring workers to migrate in accordance with the harvest calendar and the geographical location of the activities. Adding the semiproletariat peasantry to the *itinerant* fraction of the agricultural workers, a total of almost 240,000 workers share these conditions of occupational and spatial displacement. It was among these poor peasants and rural workers that the FSLN attempted to organize a revolutionary movement in the countryside. In 1978, the Rural Workers Association emerged as a result of these organizing efforts.

The Rural Workers Association, ATC

The Rural Workers Association (ATC) includes 65,000 permanent workers, organized in 37 enterprise unions in the state sector and 45 enterprise unions in the private sector.[17] The ATC campaigns for union rights, salary increases, improved working conditions, education and health benefits, technical training, an equitable food distribution system for its members, worker participation in decision-making, and higher production.

The Origins of the ATC

Under Somoza farmworkers' unions, or other organizations that threatened profits, were crushed unmercifully by the National Guard.[18] Nevertheless, in the late 1960s and early 1970s farmers and rural workers began to agitate for land and better wages. Their efforts were assisted by Sandinista Front members and Catholic activists working in the countryside. In 1969, the Jesuits, backed by the Nicaraguan bishops, established the Agrarian Promotion and Educational Center (CEPA), where peasants received workshops mainly for priests and coffee plantation workers. Those who attended these training sessions later shared their skills and helped expand social awareness within their own communities.

Influenced by CEPA's reflection/training seminars, plantation workers in Carazo and Masaya formed Committees of Agricultural Workers that demanded higher wages, decent food and housing, and sanitary facilities. In 1977, the *Asociación de Trabajadores del Campo* (Rural Workers Association, ATC) emerged from these committees. The ATC's ultimate goal was to unite all poor peasants and agricultural workers around demands for improved living conditions, year-round employment, and an end to National Guard repression in the countryside.

On April 9, 1978, the ATC demonstrated its capacity to organize peasants and rural workers by mobilizing 1,200 members and supporters in a march and hunger strike in Diriamba. Although the Guard broke up the demonstration, the march and hunger strike propelled the Association into political alignment with the FSLN. During the anti-Somoza insurrections of September 1978 and May-July 1979, the ATC proved to be a powerful force not only in building the armed struggle but in organizing political action by workers and peasants in the rural areas.

Gains and Conflicts in the ATC's First Year

During the early months after Somoza's fall the ATC organized union locals on state and private farms which included both permanent and temporary workers. And in the spring of 1980 the association fostered the creation of production cooperatives and opened its membership to thousands of small and medium peasant producers. As of July 1980, the ATC had organized almost one-third of the country's economically active rural population.[19]

Since four basic forms of production existed in the countryside, the ATC created different types of union locals to represent the state-farm workers, the private-farm workers, the small independent peasants, and the peasant cooperative members. The association then organized these local unions and base committees into municipal committees with their own elected executive councils. The national council, which set general policies for the association and selected its national executive committee, was the highest body in the ATC.[20]

The composition of the ATC demonstrated an imbalance in its strength on state and private farms: 48,712 of its members were organized in 397 credit and service cooperatives, 30,844 in 472 state farms, and 21,552 in 621 private farms.[21] In 1980, exploitation of workers often continued as before on privately-owned farms where the ATC lacked sufficient unions to fight for basic worker rights, including the implementation of minimum wage levels.[22]

On state farms, however, the ATC exercized an active presence, holding two or three political meetings a week. In many of these meetings union leaders taught the rank and file how to formulate their demands in light of the new political and economic realities in the country. On the one hand, the ATC had the difficult task of showing that the new state was not a traditional instrument of exploitation; but on the other hand, the association had to maintain its independence from the state and forcibly assert its members' demands. The ATC leadership therefore emphasized labor discipline and worker productivity to comply with the state's economic reactivation plans, but at the same time worked hard to remove uncooperative bureaucrats in various state agencies, such as the Nicaraguan Basic Foods Company, the National Development Bank, and the National Coffee Enterprise.[23]

Within the state sector, the ATC unions pushed for a variety of social services including health care, country stores, schools, and better housing. In the large, agroexporting complexes, such demands led to rapid social gains.[24] At the German Pomares sugar refinery, for example, the association gained a health clinic staffed by fourteen social workers, a commissary selling seventy-five basic products at state-controlled prices, and a production collective making clothes at no cost to the sugar workers and at little cost to their families. The ATC created union-managed stores on the state complexes to supply workers with basic goods at low prices; sixty were in operation by mid-1980. At this early date, then, the ATC had already demonstrated what strong organization could achieve.[25]

On national issues, the ATC leadership tended to advance demands only when the rank and file applied pressure. When the Worker's Front, an ultraleftist labor federation, attempted to achieve political gains by organizing sugar workers around demands for 100 percent wage hikes, the ATC did not try to compete with them. Although farmworkers averaged only 636 córdobas a month, the ATC decided to wait until higher wage demands emerged from the local affiliates. Only when this occurred in may 1980—three months after the Workers' Front conflict—did ATC executives press the Junta for wage increases.[26]

The ATC Splits

By 1980, the ATC had become an organization charged with meeting the demands of two different social classes—rural workers and agricultural producers. But lacking the capacity to resolve the often conflicting interests of the two groups, the association was unable to function effectively. As a result, in December 1980 peasant members of the ATC organized a large regional assembly in Matagalpa to build the foundation for a new peasant organization. The assembly called for a nationwide union of all small and medium producers. On April 25 and 26, 1981, 360 delegates met in Managua to form the *Union Nacional de Agricultores y Ganaderos* (National Union of Farmers and Ranchers—UNAG).[27]

The creation of UNAG meant that the ATC lost a part of its membership. Peasant producers organized in cooperatives, as well as individual peasant landowners, became members of UNAG. Permanent and seasonal agricultural workers stayed with the ATC. UNAG was thus responsible for organizing all peasant producers. The ATC was charged with organizing rural workers, and union-building became its principal task. Because a part of its membership was in work collectives, however, the ATC maintained a high degree of interest in the problems of peasant producers.

The ATC's Structure and Membership

Until 1985 the ATC organized its members into union locals on any farm that had twenty or more farmworkers. The association concentrated its organizing efforts among workers toiling on coffee, cotton, tobacco, and rice farms, as well as on cattle ranches. By early 1985 the ATC had 41,000 members organized in 450 union locals throughout the country.[28] At that time, the ATC was open to any production worker. Administrative employees in state farms, however, were affiliated with the Nicaraguan Employees Union.

In 1985 the ATC underwent a major structural change. Both the rank and file and union leaders felt that the structure was too bureaucratic and impeded worker participation in decision-making both at the workplace and in the union. Consequently, in January 1985, the ATC reorganized itself according to work sector and individual enterprise. Union members elected union executive boards in each enterprise to represent workers in negotiations with management and plan global union policies. At the same time, ATC officials at the regional level were assigned to coordinate union affairs in each agricultural sector; that is, a tobacco coordinator was designated to deal with tobacco workers' concerns, a coffee coordinator with coffee workers' interests, and so on.[29] The ATC also opened its membership to office workers and management personnel.[30] Under this new structure, the association's membership expanded to 65,000 by February 1988. These members were organized into 37 enterprise unions in the state sector and 45 enterprise unions in the private sector.[31]

The structure of the ATC parallels that of an enterprise. A union local—*seccion sindical*—exists at each UPE and at enterprise departments such as the administrative office and mechanic shop. In August 1988, nineteen union locals were functioning at Oscar Turcios: eleven on UPEs, one in the central office, one in the mechanic shop, one among central administration service workers, one in the transport department, and four at the tobacco processing facilities. Each union local consists of five secretaries: a secretary-general, a secretary of organization, a secretary of production, a secretary of labor and social affairs, and a secretary of political education and propaganda. In practice, however, union locals often function with only three or four secretaries. All union local officials are elected directly in workers' assemblies. While union local leaders do not have fixed terms of office, they are subject to immediate recall by the rank and file. Local officials ensure compliance with collective bargaining agreements, attend to workers' grievances, and report workers' concerns to the union's executive board.

Every year delegates selected by the rank and file gather in an assembly to elect the five secretaries that make up the union's executive board (*sindicato unico de la empresa*—SUE). These delegates are made up of union local activists, "vanguard" workers, and UPE supervisors and technicians. At the electoral assembly held in March 1988 one hundred delegates attended. The executive board is charged with negotiating collective bargaining agreements with management, representing the interests of rank-and-file workers at union/management meetings, assisting the work of union locals, and framing union positions on wages, incentives, and social benefits. The executive board meets every two weeks.[32]

Membership in the ATC is voluntary. Union rules state that anyone fourteen years of age or older can join the ATC. In practice, however, workers younger than fourteen who express a desire to join and understand what union membership entails are readily granted membership.[33] In February 1988, 60 percent of Oscar Turcios' 1800 employees were union members.[34] Members pay union dues of one percent of their basic wages. On many state farms that have computerized their payrolls the ATC has introduced an automatic dues deduction system. Half of the union dues are forwarded to the ATC's national office and the other half is allocated to the various union locals. Most ATC-affiliated unions have scant resources and even regional offices have difficulty securing funds for basic needs such as training seminars.[35]

The Oscar Turcios Chavarria State Farm

The Oscar Turcios Chavarria Enterprise of Tobacco, Basic Grains, and Vegetables is located in the zone of Estelí in northwestern Nicaragua. Although the enterprise devotes half of its farmland to basic grain and vegetable production, tobacco is by far its most important product. In 1987–1988, for example, tobacco production generated 91 percent of its income and employed 87 percent of its labor force.[36] Indeed, Oscar Turcios is the largest employer and principal foreign exchange earner in the region.

The Structure and Size of Oscar Turcios

Until 1983 Oscar Turcios was an extremely large enterprise, consisting of agricultural, pre-industrial, and industrial sectors. The agricultural sector comprised 6 complexes with 20 production units (Unidades de Producción Estatales—UPEs) in the zone of Jalapa and 5 complexes with 15 production units in the zone of Estelí. In addition to 5 pre-industrial facilities and a cigar factory, the enterprise possessed an administrative department and an economic studies center. During the so-called dead season when tobacco was not cultivated the enterprise employed about 3,000 people and some 5,900 during the height of the harvest season.[37]

The state farm had no sales department, designating commercial responsibilities to the enterprise director, the head of the cigar factory, and representatives of the state-run Institute for the Promotion of Exports—ENIPREX. The Ministry of Agriculture and Agrarian Reform, MIDINRA, rendered a number of services to the enterprise including long-range planning, agricultural research, the purchase of inputs, training, and auditing. This significant level of state support was vital in the early years due to the exodus of technicians that occurred after the July 1979 defeat of Somoza. In 1981 the enterprise began to receive advice from Cuban tobacco experts who carried out an extensive study of the farm's agricultural potential.[38]

Despite the considerable support it enjoyed from the Ministry of Agriculture, Oscar Turcios' size caused numerous administrative difficulties. In 1984 ministry officials decided to divide the enterprise into smaller units. The operations in Jalapa became a new enterprise named Laureano Mairena and Oscar Turcios was reduced to 12 UPEs in Estelí and Condega as well as 4 pre-industrial facilities. The cigar factories also became separate entities.[39] Despite its reduction in size, Oscar Turcios remained a large enterprise. During the 1987–1988 production cycle, the state farm planted 397 *manzanas* of tobacco and 390 *manzanas* of basic grains and vegetables, yielding 8,292 *quintales* of tobacco and 11,485 *quintales* of basic grains and vegetables.[40] Moreover, the enterprise's work force oscillated between 1,190 and 2,850 employees during the production cycle.[41]

The Production Process

The production process at Oscar Turcios has two main stages: the agricultural and the pre-industrial. The agricultural stage consists of soil preparation, transplantation of tobacco plants, cultivation of the tobacco, and the cutting of the tobacco leaves. Once cut, the tobacco is hauled to the curing sheds where the curing process begins. First, the tobacco is thread onto curing poles and then hoisted onto rafters in the curing sheds. The tobacco is heated and dried in the sheds for about 60 days and then shipped to the pre-industrial facility where a year-long curing process ensues. After the curing is completed, the tobacco leaves are classified according to their size and quality. The leaves are then packed in large bales and shipped either to the local cigar factories, a private cigarette facility, or foreign processing facilities.

The cultivation of tobacco requires extreme care during the various development stages of the plant—the sowing, transplanting, trimming, cutting, and curing stages. Once cut, tobacco leaves can be damaged if squeezed too hard by workers who pass the tobacco to the threaders. And leaves can easily be torn by threaders or workers who handle the curing poles. Leaves are also subject to damage when removed from the curing poles and tied into bundles for shipment to the processing facilities. At Oscar Turcios, careless tobacco handling has led to a steep decline in production quality. During the 1987–1988 production cycle, for example, 25 percent of the tobacco leaves suffered "mechanical damages," and only 22 percent of the crop met export quality standards.[42]

Relations with State Institutions

Until the 1988–1989 production cycle, Oscar Turcios' relations to the state were mediated by the Ministry of Agriculture and Agrarian Reform, MIDINRA. In April of each year management elaborated the state farm's technical/economic plan, based on reports from each production unit concerning raw material, machinery, and labor power needs. In June, the plan was presented to the regional office of MIDINRA which evaluated the plan and then forwarded it to the ministry's central office in Managua. The central office then approved the plan and requested financing for its implementation from the National Development Bank, BND. According to agreements with MIDINRA and the BND, Oscar Turcios was allowed to borrow up to 80 percent of its yearly budget. But due to the hyper-inflation that began in 1983, the BND loans usually amounted to only 50 percent of the total real costs of the company.[43]

Until 1986, Oscar Turcios sold its tobacco via the state-run Institute for the Promotion of Exports, ENIPREX. At the beginning of each production cycle, the enteprise communicated its production plans to ENIPREX which, in turn, developed contracts with clients, specifying quantities and prices. In 1981–1982, the state farm sold 54 percent of its tobacco leaves to the United States and the other 46 percent to Honduras.[44] After the Reagan administration imposed a trade embargo in May 1985, the enterprise began to establish commerical relations with

European markets. The majority of its tobacco sales in 1987–1988 were made to Spain, West Germany, and Belgium. Since 1985, the state farm's director, assisted by the pre-industry director and a MIDINRA national delegate, has participated directly in the commercial transactions.[45]

Until June 1988, the regional office of MIDINRA played the key role of setting guidelines for the enterprise's annual technical/economic plan and assisting the state farm in presenting its plan to the central office of the National Development Bank. To ensure advances in production quality, the ministry also provided technical assistance to Oscar Turcios via the *Dirección de Tobaco*, a technical insitute located adjacent to the farm. Moreover, the Ministry of Agriculture sells the enterprise most of its inputs, operating agricultural equipment, fertilizer, and seed stores in the city of Esteli.[46]

Oscar Turcios also maintains important relations with the Ministry of Labor, MITRAB, concerning monetary wages, worker output quotas, and health and safety regulations. To ensure medical and social security benefits for its employees, the state farm also communicates regularly with the ministries of health and social security and welfare. Since Oscar Turcios is located in a zone that has been hit by contra attacks, the enterprise works with the Ministry of Defense to coordinate plans for the armed defense of company installations.

In May 1988, the enterprise became part of the National Tobacco Corporation (Corporación Nicaragüense del Tabaco—TABANIC). The corporation was established as part of a series of major governmental economic reforms designed to streamline and decentralize the state apparatus. These reforms included a restructuring of the state agricultural sector with the aim of "establishing a correct division of labor among the different sectoral institutions, producers, enterprises, and organizations responsible for administering production."[47] According to the decree establishing TABANIC, the corporation was charged with "directing, organizing, administering, and promoting . . . the functioning of state enterprises in the tobacco agro-industrial sector and in those activities connected to that sector."[48] Equipped with its own work teams and budget, the corporation took over many of the former tasks of MIDINRA: soliciting equipment for Oscar Turcios, helping the enterprise establish its annual economic/technical plan, and obtaining financing for the company. By mid-1988 the president of TABANIC was participating in Oscar Turcios' marketing efforts. Citing TABANIC's independence, legal powers, and convenient location in Esteli, the enterprise director was confident that the corporation would improve the state farm's dealings with the government.[49]

Administrative Problems

Given the contra war, the United States economic embargo, the shortage of trained administrators and technicians, and the dependent nature of its economy, running any state enterprise in Nicaragua is extremely difficult.[50] Oscar Turcios faces a myriad of administrative problems all of which have hampered its efforts to become a consistently profitable enterprise. The trade embargo imposed on Nicaragua by the Reagan administration in May 1985 had a major impact on the state farm's tobacco sales. Until that date the enterprise sold the bulk of its tobacco to the United States. Although it has established new markets in Europe, the additional transportation costs make these markets less than ideal.[51] The uncontrollable inflation that has raged in Nicaragua since 1984 has also burdened the enterprise with serious difficulties. The impossibility of anticipating future expenses because of rapid price increases have made efficient economic planning almost impossible.[52] Spiralling costs have also led the to scarcity of key inputs required by the enterprise. The state farm's services director outlines the consequences of such scarcity:

> The scarcity of products and materials in the local market means that we have to mobilize a purchase team at the national level. This implies personnel and transportation costs above the cost of the required products. . . . Much time is spent searching for products because several trips are often required to obtain just one product or spare part indispensable for production.[53]

A combination of problems also plagues the transport fleet and the company's machine and mechanical shop. Many vehicles are parked in the repair shop for lack of spare parts or because the mechanics lack the know-how to repair the vehicles. Deficiencies in coordinating the use of vehicles has also hampered the enterprise; many vehicles are overburdened with use, while others are underutilized. And due to the insufficient number of vehicles, the enterprise is sometimes forced to rent transportation services, raising production costs.[54] Many problems also exist in the maintenance of the company's agricultural machinery. Tractors, irrigation equipment, and fumigation units are often out of commission because of poor maintenance. Moreover, many mechanics have left their jobs on the state farm in search of higher incomes in the informal sector, reducing drastically the number of trained mechanics in the machine shop.[55]

Another set of administrative problems arises from the contra war. Like other state farms in the region, Oscar Turcios has suffered direct damages as a result of contra attacks on the company's production units.

The most damaging incident occurred in October 1987, when a contra force hit the San Ramon UPE, burning three curing sheds, a jeep, and a tractor. The contras killed four civilians in the attack. Three months later, in January 1988, 60 counterrevolutionaries struck the Arenal UPE, attempting once again to destroy infrastructure on the state farm. Fortunately, the arrival of artillery units from a nearby army base prevented most of the contras from penetrating the farm. But the contras managed to cause some damage to houses and a school located in a new community project on the production unit. The contras also murdered a 12-year-old boy and the president of an agricultural cooperative located just above the Arenal UPE.

Both contra attacks led to increased security measures throughout the state farm. Worker militia units were forced to spend sleepless nights guarding vulnerable UPES, thus reducing their day-time energies. And since managers and union leaders participated in many defense planning sessions, time that could have been spent in production planning and union organizing was lost.[56]

Labor Power Shortages

"We need 500 more workers if we are to harvest the entire tobacco crop by April. And I simply don't know how we will be able to hire that many more workers." That was the director of production at Oscar Turcios reporting to a February 1987 enterprise meeting the bad news of labor shortages. Moreover, according to the director of human resources, the enterprise needs 3,300 workers during the December-April peak period, but in the 1986–87 harvest season the state farm employed an average of only 2,664 workers.[57] The figures for 1987–88 were even worse; the average number of workers during that harvest season was only 2,013.[58] In both the 1985–86 and 1986–87 production cycles the shortage of workers resulted in a late tobacco harvest, and a late harvest means lower yields and higher costs.

One reason for the serious shortage of workers in tobacco and other sectors of Nicaragua's agriculture is the very success of the nation's agrarian reform. Because tens of thousands of peasants have benefitted from the agrarian reform, many of them no longer need to sell their labor power during the harvest season; land entitlements, improvements in commercializaton, and credit and technical assistance have created economic conditions that permit small peasants to remain on their farms year-round. In addition, many members of the semi-proletariat have received financing for cultivating their small plots of land, and no longer need to work in the harvest. The agrarian reform has also created more possibilities for permanent wage employment through agricultural projects in tobacco, milk, sugar, African palm, rice, and corn. Consequently, there are fewer temporary workers available during the harvest season.

Second, since inflation began to skyrocket in 1984, many Nicaraguans have discovered that they can earn much more in commercial activity, so-called non-productive work. For example, a person who can put together a wooden cart, buy a block of ice, and obtain sweetened food colorings to sell snow cones at a Sunday afternoon baseball game in Managua, can make more money in one day than from a week's work on a coffee farm. Even more profitable is reselling toiletries brought in from neighboring countries. In 1987 a woman from Estelí told me that after seven years in tobacco harvests she had quit her job to sell fruit drinks to her neighbors. Given these economic conditions, many traditional workers have migrated to the cities and others who live in rural towns have entered commercial activities, further straining labor power needs in agriculture.

Finally, fewer workers are available for the harvests because of the intensive military mobilization of traditional farmworkers that began during the 1983–1984 harvest. For example, in Region VI, 40 percent of the ATC-affiliated workers, 5,000 out of 12,000, volunteered for defense duties during the 1983–1984 harvest cycle.[59] Furthermore, when male members of the family enlist for military duty, the other family members usually fail to join the harvest campaigns, thereby adding to the labor power shortage.

A more disturbing reason why it is ever more difficult to find enough workers for the harvests—and even for year-round farm work—is increasingly unattractive wages. True, before the revolution, the official minimum wage was seldom paid to agricultural workers, especially women. Now, however, the minimum wage is enforced—largely because workers are no longer afraid to speak up and are widely organized in ATC locals. Indeed, the ATC's first post-Somoza demand called for a government-enforced minimum wage. In 1980, the Ministry of Labor established a minimum wage of 25.30 córdobas per day.[60] The ATC also insisted that women farmworkers receive equal pay for equal work. Although the government declared a comparable-worth policy shortly after July 1979, the Labor Ministry failed to enforce it until the creation of the National System of Ordering Work and Salaries in 1984.

It is true as well that for some time workers' declining purchasing power was partially offset by a "social wage" in the form of free health and educational services. Fringe benefits probably covered the decline in purchasing power from 1980 through 1982. Since then inflation has sharply eroded its effect. Moreover, the government-provided benefits are increasingly undermined by the economic crisis engendered by foreign aggression. Defense spending comprised only 7 percent of the national budget in 1980 and 1981. But it increased to 13 percent in 1982, 19 percent in 1983, 25 percent in 1984, 45 percent in 1985, and 50 percent in 1986. These increases have forced cutbacks in health and education facilities. The cutbacks lower the "social wage" of all workers, agricultural and otherwise. The decreases, however, are more keenly felt in the countryside where cash earnings tend to be significantly lower.

Agricultural wages that buy less and less not only do not attract workers but also tend to erode the incentive for better worker productivity. Consequently, more workers are needed to do the same amount of work, worsening the labor shortage. In the case of tobacco, a large percentage of manual labor is done by children whose output is far below that of adult workers. Since low incomes cause so much desertion from state farms I will examine Sandinista wage policy in detail.

The Monetary Wage

Class relations in Nicaragua since the triumph have been marked by sharp conflicts over monetary wages. During the early "reconstructionist" stage of the revolution (1979–1982), the revolutionary state tended to respond to workers' demands through consumption subsidies and expansion of social services—what in that period was called the *social wage*—more than through an increase in monetary wages. These social benefits probably covered the decline in purchasing power from 1980 through 1982. But by 1983 rising inflation and the economic crisis engendered by foreign aggression had undermined the government-provided subsidies and social wage. Consequently, workers began to demand significant wage increases.

Through 1983, however, the government continued to officially bar wage hikes for all workers. Sandinista leaders argued that until Nicaragua could afford to import more goods, wage and salary increases would be "demagogic" since more money in the hands of workers would just fuel inflation and leave the workers in the same position as before. As Comandante Tomás Borge told workers demanding higher wages at the Pedro Rivas Recalde state farm:

Let's suppose that each of you earns 1,000 córdobas a month, and we decide to double that to 2,000. What would happen? There would be more money on the street. Isn't that so? So the goods we have would be bought up very quickly, with more money around, and we would start to have shortages. And when shortages start, things begin to get more expensive. So that within a short time your 2,000 córdobas would buy the same that 1,000 córdobas bought before.[61]

The Sandinista leadership's arguments, however, failed to appease the workers. After an outbreak of (illegal) strike activity in 1982 following a wage freeze and a substantial drop in purchasing power of wages in 1983, the government bowed to political "realism" and by mid-1983 began steps to raise wages. The first step was to complete plans to overhaul the wage and salary scale. The government was determined to institute the principle of equal pay for equal work, thereby overcoming the anarchic salary system inherited from Somoza. Over the years a person doing one type of activity on one farm received significantly more than someone on another farm doing the same work. For example, some technicians who worked for wealthy landowners earned as much as 30,000 córdobas a year, while others earned only 7,000. Many unskilled workers earned only 210 córdobas per month, while an owner's favorite employee received as much as 1,200 córdobas per month. In addition, women farm workers never earned as much as their male counterparts in the same jobs.[62]

The goal of the new wage scale, then, was to create a fair salary scale based on the specific tasks that workers perform. Special commissions organized according to the country's different economic sectors developed the *Sistema Nacional de Organización del Trabajo y los Salarios* (National System of Ordering Work and Salaries—SNOTS). Each commission included management representatives, union leaders, Ministry of Labor officials, and experienced workers and technicians. The commission members first organized workshops to train each other in how to devise the new system in their respective sectors. Next, they determined a work plan that included the number of businesses in each sector, the total number of occupations, and the sector's occupational breakdown. The commissions then formed sub-commissions to establish job descriptions and salary scales. Defining each occupation according to its work functions, the sub-commissions analyzed its degree of complexity in order to place it within a salary scale. After setting the value of each occupation, they submitted the new salary scale to the workers for their review and approval. Finally, the sector's management representatives, Ministry of Labor officials, and union leaders signed the salary accords.[63]

In addition to defining job categories in terms of difficulty, level of training, and required experience, the SNOTS program implemented a "norm system" which attempts to establish a daily or weekly goal that a worker should be able to achieve if he/she works diligently and with little resource waste. Once a norm is established a worker can receive a wage bonus as an incentive for surpassing the norm. But setting norms has proven to be an immensely difficult task, especially in the industrial sector where spare parts are lacking and power shortages frequent.

Moreover, establishing norms requires meticulous analysis by technicians already overburdened with other tasks.[64]

The universal salary scale established under the SNOTS program helped to order salaries. The standardization of job categories and pay eliminated much of the chaos that previously reigned in the wage labor sector and the SNOTS program guaranteed equity in pay increases whenever they occurred. In 1985 the government granted three wage increases totalling 107 percent, and in the first three months of 1986 alone workers received two wage increases totalling almost 140 percent. Although these increases lagged considerably behind inflation, workers at least knew that they were applied fairly since the wage scales were widely disseminated.

In 1987, however, the SNOTS system came under heavy pressure from most workers and many private and public sector managers. Inflation that year reached an astounding 1,300 percent and the periodic pay increases failed to recoup workers' purchasing power. Indeed, many workers were unable to buy the basic goods package and many private owners and state managers complained that the government-controlled wage system failed to encourage companies to be more productive. By the end of 1987, managers and professionals were clamoring to be taken off the SNOTS program. Although they lost this demand, many were reclassified to higher levels in the SNOTS salary scale and managers and professionals in the highest levels were granted access to durable consumer goods with enticing credit terms.

Finally, on February 12, 1988, in a surprise move, the government announced a monetary reform. It created a new córdoba equivalent to 1000 old córdobas, set one universal exchange rate, reduced the money supply, and re-established the true value of imports. The government also adjusted the prices of the items on the basic market basket list, which now contained 46 products, and set a new minimum wage of 500 córdobas and a maximum of 7530.[65]

Although the February measures included a substantial salary increase of some 400 percent, the measures abolished a range of incentives which had been growing during 1986 and 1987 and which averaged 90 percent more than the basic salary in the productive sector. Table 1.1 shows that although the actual increase in base salaries in the productive sector was less than 400 percent, this rise was at least a temporary relief for the working class. Nevertheless, the table shows that coordinators and managers received wage increases between 421 and 622 percent. At the same time, the salary scale, which previously had a range of eight times between the bottom salary and the top one, was liberalized in favor of the higher wages. The difference between the top and bottom incomes is now 15 to 1.

TABLE 1.1   Salary Increase Differences between December 1987
and March 1988

Salary Scale	December 1987[a]	March 1988[a]	Increase (%)
Basic Salary Levels			
1 (Minimum)	123.5	500	305
9 (Maximum for a worker)	305.6	1,380	352
16 (Average urban)	447.0	2,440	446
39 (General director)	988.1	7,530	662
Productive Sector			
Total Salary[b]			
1 (Minimum)	234.8	650	177
9 (Maximum for a worker)	580.6	1,794	209
16 (Average urban)	849.3	3,172	274
39 (General director)	1,877.2	9,786	421
Non-productive Sector			
Total Salary[c]			
1 (Minimum)	173.0	525	204
9 (Maximum for a worker)	427.8	1,449	239
16 (Average urban)	625.8	2,562	309
39 (General director)	1,383.4	7,907	472

[a] In new cordobas.

[b] Incentives for salaries in the productive sector calculated as
90% of the basic salary in December 1987 and 30% of the basic
salary on March 12, 1988.

[c] Incentives for salaries in the non-productive sector calculated
at 40% of the basic salary in December 1987 and 5% of the basic
salary on March 12, 1988 (average service of two years).

Source: Instituto Historico Centroamericano, Envio, (April 1988),
p. 29.

Many economic observers argue that the disproportionate raises given professionals were necessary to slow the desertion of professionals to the informal sector. For example, the *Envio*, a monthly published by the Central American Historical Institute, asserted:

> The distortion in the balance between salaries in the formal sector and prices meant a permanent temptation for workers to move to the informal sector, a temptation particularly strong for professionals. Workers at the top end of the scale who left the formal sector began selling their services at inflated prices to that same formal sector, but now as free agents in their informal sector mini-establishments. It was to avoid that dangerous phenomenon that the differential in salaries was increased.[66]

According to government estimates, the new average urban salary of 2,562 córdobas (level 16 on the SNOTS scale) would buy the basic

TABLE 1.2   Real Purchasing Power of a 2-Salary Income for a
Family of 6

Products	Daily Ration Purchased[a]	Monthly Cost[b]
Rice	.33 lbs.	246.00
Beans	.25 lbs.	258.75
Sugar	.12 lbs.	86.40
Oil	.1 pint	108.00
Tortilla	1 unit	211.20
Bread	.16 lbs.	307.50
Pinolillo	.16 lbs.	157.50
Coffee	.03 lbs.	135.00
Laundry soap	2 units/week per family	47.20
Matches	1 box/week per family	2.40
Bath soap	1 unit/week per family	20.40
Bus tickets	24/week for two workers	48.00
Total		1,609.55

[a]Families unable to buy proteins eat more cereals than the
rations calculated in the minimum market basket.
[b]Official prices as of March 10, 1988 in new cordobas.
Source: Instituto Historico Centroamericano, Envio, (April 1988),
p. 30.

market basket of 46 goods. It was also projected that there are an
average of 2.2 workers per family, which indicated that those in the
middle income ranges would be able to buy much more than the basic
basket of goods. But, according to those same projections, the maximum
basic salary for a worker (level 9) would only cover about 60 percent
of the basic market basket. Table 1.2 shows that a family of six with
the man earning a level 6 wage (1,012 córdobas) and the woman a level
3 wage (792 córdobas) would be able to purchase 12 basic products.
The combined wages would buy a subsistence diet in which there is
no meat, eggs, milk, chicken, vegetables, fruit, or pasta, nor would it
purchase clothes, domestic utensils, school supplies, toilet paper, toothpaste, or sanitary pads.

The *Envio* ends its analysis of the February reforms' impact on wages
by concluding that "even after the new measures, the distortion in the
relationship of salaries to prices leaves the informal sector looking
extremely attractive. The new economic package is not a magic wand
and there is likely to be no solution to the crisis for several years."[67]

Indeed, the economic situation continued to deteriorate during the
months following the February reforms. Inflation surged forward at a
50 percent clip a month and no wage increases were granted in March,
April, and May. Finally, on June 14, Daniel Ortega announced a series

of free-market policies designed to control inflation and protect workers. The government approved a 30 percent wage increase and a more flexible national salary system. Although base wages continue to be set according to a universal scale based on qualifications and experience, the new policy allows profitable companies to give their workers raises, new benefits, or basic supplies. In all cases the incentives must be based on productivity and production in order to reduce the impact higher wages could have on the amount of money in circulation. Central government and service sector employees are excluded from these provisions.[68]

It is obvious from this summary of the monetary wage system that the state farm functions in a rapidly changing economic context. Buffeted by a crisis-ridden economy, both management and workers face formidable obstacles in their attempt to transform the enterprise's production relations. The nature of this attempt is the subject of the remaining chapters.

Notes

1. CEPAL, *Nicaragua: Antecedentes economicos del proceso revolucionario* (CEPAL, 1979).

2. John A. Booth, *The End and the Beginning: The Nicaraguan Revolution* (Boulder, Colorado: Westview Press, 1982), p. 201.

3. The rest of this section draws from Richard Harris, "The Role of Industry in Revolutionary Nicaragua's Mixed Economy," in Richard Harris and Carlos M. Vilas eds., *Nicaragua: A Revolution under Siege* (London: Zed Press, 1985).

4. Quoted in ibid, p. 41.

5. Richard Dellobuono, "Nicaragua's Emergency Laws: An In-Depth Look," *Nicaraguan Perspectives* 3 (Winter 1982), p. 10.

6. Goran Therborn's phrase, in *What Does the Ruling Class Do When It Rules?* (London: New Left Books, 1978), p. 146.

7. Jaime Wheelock, *El gran desafio* (Managua: Editorial Nueva Nicaragua, 1983), p. 102.

8. Eduardo Baumeister, "The Structure of Nicaraguan Agriculture and the Sandinista Agrarian Reform," in Richard Harris and Carlos M. Vilas, eds., *Nicaragua: A Revolution Under Siege* (London: Zed Books Ltd., 1985), p. 11.

9. Quoted in Joseph Collins, *What Difference Could a Revolution Make? Food and Farming in the New Nicaragua* (San Francisco: Institute for Food and Development Policy, 1986), p. 60.

10. The following account of the INRA system draws on Dilling et al., *Nicaragua: A People's Revolution* (Washington: EPICA Task Force, 1980), p. 82, and Deere and Marchetti, "The Worker-Peasant Alliance in the First Year of the Nicaraguan Agrarian Reform," *Latin American Perspectives* 8 (Spring 1981), p. 53.

11. Carmen Diana Deere el al., "Agrarian Reform and the Transition in Nicaragua: 1979–1983," (unpublished mimeo, November 1983), pp. 5–6.

12. Orlando Nuñez Soto, "The Third Social Force in National Liberation Movements," *Latin American Perspectives* 29 (Spring 1981), p. 11.

13. Carmen Diana Deere and Peter Marchetti, "The Worker-Peasant Alliance in the First Year of the Nicaraguan Agrarian Reform," *Latin American Perspectives* 29 (Spring 1981), p. 49.

14. Carlos M. Vilas, *The Sandinista Revolution: National Liberation and Social Transformation in Central America* (New York: Monthly Review Press, 1986), p. 61.

15. Ibid., p. 63.

16. Ibid.

17. Heliette Ehlers, "La organización de los trabajadores, un proceso no acabado," *El Machete* (February 1988), p. 11.

18. This section draws on Dilling et al., *Nicaragua: A People's Revolution*, pp. 23–26.

19. George Black, *Triumph of the People* (London: Zed Press, 1981), pp. 272–273.

20. David Kaimowitz and Joseph R. Thome, "Nicaragua's Agrarian Reform: The First Year," in Thomas T. Walker, ed. *Nicaragua in Revolution* (New York: Praeger, 1982), p. 237.

21. George Black, *Triumph of the People* (London: Zed Press, 1981), p. 272.

22. Ibid., p. 273.

23. Ibid., p. 274.

24. Deere and Marchetti, "The Worker-Peasant Alliance," p. 60.

25. Black, *Triumph of the People*, p. 274.

26. Ibid.

27. Matilde Zimmerman, "How Sandinistas Won Over the Nicaraguan Farmers," *Intercontinental Press* (April 20, 1981), p. 391.

28. Ehlers, "La organización de los trabajadores," p. 11.

29. Ibid.

30. The opening of the ATC to administrative workers occurred in May 1985 after the country's pro-Sandinista union federations decided that only one federation should represent employees at each worksite.

31. Ehlers, "La organizacion de los trabajadores," p. 11.

32. Interview with Eligio Castellano, SUE member, January 8, 1988.

33. Interview with Vivian Perez, secretary general of enterprise union, September 9, 1986.

34. Interview with Vivian Perez, secretary general of enterprise union, March, 1988.

35. Interview with Alberto Martinez, ATC secretary of organization in Region I, August 10, 1987.

36. Oscar Turcios Chavarria, *Informe Evaluativo Ciclo 87–88 Avance Ciclo 88–89*, July 6, 1988, pp. 13, 18.

37. Eduardo Gomez, *Tabaco Nicaragüense* (Managua: INCAE, 1983), p. 5.

38. Ibid.

39. Interview with Rene Boniche, enterprise technician, February 1987.

40. Oscar Turcios, "*Informe Evaluativo: Ciclo 87–88, Avance Ciclo 88–89*," July 6, 1988, pp. 4, 7. One *manzana* equals 1.86 acres and one *quintal* equals 100 pounds.

41. Interview with Berta Rugama, labor force technician, August 1988.

42. Oscar Turcios, *Informe Evaulativo: Ciclo, 87–88*, p. 6.

43. Interview with Hector Valdivia, enterprise director, August 1988.

44. Gomez, *Tabaco Nicaragüense*, pp. 21–22.

45. Interview with Hector Valdivia, enterprise director; August 1988.

46. Ibid.

47. MIDINRA, *Plan de Trabajo: Balance y Perspectivas 1988* (Managua: MIDINRA, 1988), p. 36.

48. *La Gaceta—Diario Oficial, Ley de la Corporación Nicaragüense del Tabaco, Decreto No. 359*, May 31, 1988, pp. 612–613.

49. Interview with Hector Valdivia, enterprise director, August 17, 1988.

50. For a helpful discussion on the problem of finding and developing capable managers for Nicaragua's state sector, see James E. Austin and John C. Ickis, "Management, Managers, and Revolution," *World Development* Vol. 14, No. 7 (1986), pp. 777–779.

51. Ulises Gutierrez, *Problemas de la Gestión Administrativa de la Empresa Oscar Turcios Chavarria de la Region I Las Segovias*, CIERA MIDINRA, December, 1986, p. 7.

52. Ibid., p. 9.

53. Ibid., pp. 8–9.

54. Ibid., p. 11.

55. Ibid., p. 13.

56. In January and February 1988 I attended a number of defense planning sessions and witnessed firsthand the draining effects that defense efforts entail for enterprise employees.

57. Oscar Turcios Chavarria, *Informe Ciclo 86–87*, July 1987.

58. Interview with Berta Rugama, labor force technician, August 1988.

59. *El Machete*, April 1984, p. 5.

60. *El Machete*, November 1983, p. 2.

61. Quoted in Collins, *What Difference Could a Revolution Make*, p. 69.

62. *El Machete*, November 1983, p. 3.

63. *Trabajadores*, February 1984, p. 3.

64. For an excellent discussion of how the norm system was introduced into Nicaragua, see Richard Stahler-Scholk, *La normación del Trabajo en Nicaragua, 1983–1986*, CRIES, Managua, October 1985.

65. *Barricada Internacional*, July 13, 1988, p. 13.

66. Instituto Historico Centroamericano, "Economic Reform: Taking it to the Streets," *Envio*, Volume 7 Number 82 (April 1988), pp. 29–30.

67. Ibid., pp. 30–31.

68. *Barricada Internacional*, June 30, 1988, p. 7.

Class Relations

Three fundamental observations must be made before beginning an analysis of the enterprise's class relations. First, I make no bones about contending that exploitation relations continue to exist in Nicaragua's state sector. This chapter will show that whether one considers inequalities in production assets or income variations, significant differences—*class differences*—exist among the employees at Oscar Turcios. Second, although exploitation relations prevail in Nicaraguan state enterprises, the rate of exploitation is considerably lower than that found in "actually existing socialism." Whether this is due to Nicaragua's underdevelopment, income ceilings, worker participation, or other concrete aspects of the Sandinista revolution, is subject to debate. Whatever the explanation, a careful analysis of class relations in Nicaragua's public sector shows that exploitative relations are less intense in this young revolution than in developed socialist countries. Third, the transformation in production relations on state enterprises has eliminated the gross forms of exploitation that reigned under the Somoza dictatorship. Indeed, many economists partially attribute the state sector's relatively low productivity rate to the abolition of Somocista oppression.

The Class Structure of Oscar Turcios

The Managerial Class

In determining membership in the managerial class, I have followed Wright's claim that managers can be distinguished by their control of organization assets. Wright defines organization assets as follows:

> Organization assets consist in the effective control over the coordination and integration of the division of labour. Typically, such assets are particularly salient in defining the exploitation relations of management, although not all jobs which are formally labelled "managers" involve control over organization assets. Some "manager" jobs may simply be

37

technical experts who provide advice to the effective controllers of organizational planning and coordination. In the terms of the exploitation-centred concept of class, such "managers" might be credential exploiters, but not organization-exploiters.[1]

At Oscar Turcios the enterprise director and top management—the individual department directors—all exploit organization assets. Each of these positions involves control over the coordination and integration of the company's division of labor. For instance, the departmental head of agricultural production is charged with "directing, coordinating, supervising, planning, and controlling all activities pertaining to the enterprise's agricultural production, participating in the elaboration of the company's technical–economic plan and production plans."[2] It is noteworthy that the director of production must hold a degree in agronomy and possess at least five years experience in tobacco cultivation.[3]

The state farm's director of human resources also holds a managerial position. According to the occupational description of this position, the director of human resources "participates in the Enterprise Consultative Council and gives orientations on all issues concerning employment, work organization and salaries, occupational safety and health, labor power requirements, and job training." Moreover, the human resources director "elaborates and evaluates the department's work plans in terms of the problematic and characteristics of the enterprise."[4] Job requirements for this position include the completion of courses on the SNOTS program and prior experience in the field of human resources.[5]

At the complex level of the enterprise the one position that is clearly a management position is that of "complex director." This occupation's job description matches Wright's definition of managerial positions: "positions which are directly involved in making policy decisions within the workplace and which have effective authority over subordinates."[6] According to the complex director's occupational description, the holder of this position "elaborates, in conjunction with the production director, the annual production plans; supervises . . . the fulfillment of production activities; supervises and evaluates the complex's economic plans in coordination with the complex administrators. . . ."[7] To obtain the position of complex director one must be an agronomical engineer with at least three years experience. The completion of a course in enterprise administration is also required.[8]

In addition to the enterprise director, the director of production, the director of human resources, and the three complex directors, there are six more managers at Oscar Turcios: the directors of the economic, accounting, and administration departments, the processing facility director, the director of the potato program, and the director of the basic grains and vegetable program.

The Coordinators

As an intermediate class, the coordinators are difficult to classify. Generally speaking, coordinators in Nicaragua's state sector include those positions which Wright designates as "supervisors" and "experts." Unlike managers, coordinators have marginal or no organization assets. Thus, Wright defines supervisors as "positions which have effective authority over subordinates, but are not involved in organizational decision-making."[9] For the most part, coordinators are credential-exploiters; that is, coordinators must possess certain formal credentials in order to perform their jobs. Since many job titles and occupational designations are extremely vague with respect to the credentials they demand, one must use a combination of occupational titles, formal credentials, and job traits to distinguish people in jobs where certain credentials are mandatory—and thus positions involving credential asset exploitation—from those not in such jobs.

One coordinator position that clearly exploits credentials, but not organization assets, is that held by UPE technical supervisors. While it is tempting to regard these technicians as managers, Wright's admonition concerning certain "manager" jobs is warranted here: "Some 'manager' jobs may simply be technical experts who provide advice to the effective controllers of organizational planning and coordination."[10] In Oscar Turcios, the complex directors are the "effective controllers of organizational planning and coordination." Thus one of the primary responsibilities of a technical supervisor is to "provide periodic reports to his immediate supervisor concerning the development of activities carried out in the production unit."[11]

Two groups of coordinators work in the "central administration" of the company.[12] One group consists of credential exploiters: personnel who calculate costs and/or gather statistics for their department heads. The technician "C" in labor resources, for example, must "maintain statistical control of the biweekly and monthly labor force . . . study the rate of labor force turnover . . . maintain records of workers' performances, and keep track of workers' vacation time."[13] This technician is required to have an accounting degree, have completed courses related to the position, and have at least two years of experience.[14] The other group of central administration coordinators supervise the different institutions that provide services to the company. The commissary administrator, for instance, "oversees the procurement of basic products and complementary goods, delivers them to the commissary warehouse, elaborates plans to distribute supplies throughout the enterprise, and supervises the sales and accounting procedures."[15] The holder of this position must be a commercial accountant with two or more years of experience.[16]

On Oscar Turcios, and throughout Nicaragua's state sector, many people who occupy coordinator positions do not possess university degrees but have attended special training courses in their fields and/ or have years of experience in their speciality. Thus most UPE supervisors and assistant supervisors lack formal credentials, but possess considerable expertise in the tobacco production process as a result of many years of work experience. An UPE assistant supervisor "under the instructions of the UPE supervisor, supervises, controls, and directs the work carried out in each cultivation phase; verifies that groups supervisors receive quality work performed by the workers according to technical instructions."[17] The UPE assistant supervisor oversees the work of between three and seven group leaders during the harvest season. The job requirements include at least three years experience in tobacco cultivation and experience in personnel supervision.[18]

The Working Class

The working class in Oscar Turcios includes all non-supervisory manual laborers plus "proletarianized" white-collar workers. The bulk of the enterprise's working-class employees labor in the 13 production units as field workers engaged in the planting, cultivating, and harvesting of vegetables and tobacco. The state farm administration calls these employees *obreros manuales*—manual workers—and distinguishes them according to whether they perform jobs with norms or without norms.[19] In addition to field workers, some 300 manual workers participate in one or another tobacco processing job. During a one-year period many workers may perform at least two separate manual jobs—one in the field and one involving processing. For example, most of the women in the tobacco processing facility spend a month or more cultivating corn and beans on the UPEs and three months passing or threading tobacco in the curing sheds. Once the tobacco has been prepared for the curing process, these women return to their job stations in the processing facility.

Another group of manual workers carry out jobs related to the operation or maintenance of the state farm's machinery. These workers include the tractor and truck drivers, and the mechanics who maintain vehicles. Most of these workers are viewed as skilled workers and receive higher wages than fieldworkers and tobacco processors. In addition to these transport workers, more than 200 workers on the farm perform administrative and service tasks. On production units administrative and service workers include the norm checkers, warehouse clerks, payroll clerks, security guards, cooks, and janitors. In the central office, these workers include the secretaries, records clerks, cashiers, and purchasing agents.

Although the overwhelming majority of working class positions at Oscar Turcios are held by manual workers, the manual workers on the state farm are by no means homogenous. They can be classified into two major groups: skilled and unskilled manual workers. I call "skilled" manual work on the state farm any job that requires a special training course and/or at least one year of training before a worker is able to reach the task's required norm. Employing this definition, skilled manual work would include such obvious tasks as tractor driving and mechanical repair, as well as certain tasks that management currently regards as unskilled, such as tobacco threading and fumigation.

Administrative and service workers at Oscar Turcios can also be divided into those that are skilled and unskilled. In each complex, for example, payroll clerks who monitor the daily productivity of UPE employees are regarded as skilled administrative workers, while the warehouse clerks and norm checkers are viewed as relatively unskilled. In the central administrative office, executive secretaries and purchasing agents are considered skilled white-collar workers, while file clerks and secretaries are seen as unskilled. Among service workers, carpenters and electricians who maintain the company's infrastructure are paid higher wages than cooks and gardeners. Indeed, most skilled service workers, although manual laborers, receive higher wages than field-workers and tobacco processors.

The Monetary Wage

The monetary wage plays a major role in class relations on the state farm. Income questions provoke extended discussions in union meetings and union-management forums. Given the galloping inflationary spiral faced by wage and salary employees since 1983, all the company's employees—workers, coordinators, and managers—strive to increase their earnings in the vain attempt to keep pace with inflation. This class competition takes place within parameters set by the state and enterprise bodies that regulate income matters. We begin an analysis of the state farm's wage and salary structure by examining the workings of the SNOTS program within the enterprise.

The SNOTS System at Oscar Turcios

Since 1983 the monetary wage system at Oscar Turcios has been based on the National System of Ordering Work and Salaries, SNOTS. In that year, the company began to implement the SNOTS program by forming study circles involving the union locals in the three processing facilities.[20] These study circles were charged with familiarizing themselves with the new policies associated with the SNOTS program. The enterprise then established a SNOTS commission made up of personnel from the human resources department, technicians, and union leaders. Regional officials from the Ministry of Labor, the Ministry of Agriculture, and the ATC lent their assistance to the enterprise commission. The commission's principal task was to develop comprehensive job descriptions of the numerous tasks performed on the state farm.

In April 1984 the SNOTS commission completed its evaluation of the jobs held by manual workers in agriculture and pre-industry. The commission evaluated each job according to its complexity, level of responsibility, and degree of supervision. In September 1984 the commission evaluated service and administrative jobs and in January 1985 surveyed technical and top management positions. Technicians and directors were assigned salaries according to their position in the enterprise's administrative hierarchy, their expertise, their responsibilities, the number of their subordinates, and the importance of their work sphere.

Thus by early 1985 the enterprise had established a comprehensive break-down of its division of labor and had assigned salaries according to the national salary scale. Table 2.1 depicts the occupational structure that the SNOTS program engendered on Oscar Turcios' agricultural production complexes.

Significant income differentials exist within the company's occupational hierarchy. An analysis of employees' earnings on complex 3 and the central office during the two pay periods from December 12, 1987 to January 20, 1988 reveals the precise degree of the differences in earnings among the enterprise's three classes. The 196 working-class employees earned an average of 259,000 córdobas a month.[21] Income differentials among these workers varied considerably, ranging from the 169,000 córdobas a month earned by most tobacco threaders and passers to 702,164 córdobas earned by one tractor driver. This differential of four to one is largely due to the considerable overtime and incentives earned by tractor drivers.[22] But the study shows significant earnings variations even among workers in the same jobs. One tractor driver, who performed little overtime and earned no incentives during the four-week pay period, earned only 389,222 córdobas—nearly half the income of the best-paid

TABLE 2.1 Occupational Structure on Oscar Turcios' Production
Complex #3 in July 1988.

Occupation	SNOTS Level	Number of Employees
Complex Director	30	1
Technical Supervisor	26	3
Complex Accountant	23	1
Unit Supervisor "A"	20	4
Complex Payroll Supervisor	18	1
Agricultural Machinery Supervisor	17	1
Unit Assistant Supervisor "A"	15	1
Payroll Clerk "A"	15	3
Tractor Driver "A"	14	11
Mechanic "A"	16	1
Office Clerk "A"	12	4
Fumigation Supervisor	11	4
Group Supervisor "A"	11	8
Group Supervisor "B"	10	2
Carpenter "A"	10	1
Kitchen Supervisor	9	4
Commissary Clerk "A"	9	1
Tobacco Curer	8	4
Security Guard	8	10
Tobacco Threader	8	30
Tobacco Passer	8	25
Tobacco Hoister	8	60
Norm Checker	8	5
Tobacco Aligner	8	10
Equipment Handler	7	5
Kitchen Aide	6	8

tractor driver. And the highest-earning group leader received 518,565 córdobas, almost 50 percent more than the lowest-paid group leader.

The 14 coordinators in complex 3 earned an average of 729,000 córdobas during January.[23] The range of incomes among these employees was narrower than the income range among workers. The lowest paid UPE assistant supervisor earned 552,981 córdobas, while the complex accountant earned 881,898 córdobas, a differential of 1.6 to 1. Since coordinators in each occupation received the same incentive bonus during this pay period, the variations in income among holders of the same job were negligible. The only manager in the complex—the complex director—earned 1,033,544 córdobas, an income four times greater than the average workers' income and 1.4 times more than the average coordinators' income.

The six managers in the central office earned an average salary of 1,222,000 córdobas in the pay period studied, ranging from the director's

1,707,542 córdobas to the 1,101,684 earned by the director of human resources. The 19 coordinators in the central administration office earned an average of 763,000 córdobas, just 4.5 percent more than the average salary earned by coordinators in complex 3. The highest paid coordinator earned one and a half times more than the lowest paid coordinator. Wages earned by the 24 workers employed in the central office differed markedly from those of their counterparts on the production unit. The white-collar workers earned an average of 445,000 córdobas, 1.7 times more than the average wage of the mostly blue-collar workers in complex three. The wage range between the central office workers was more than 2 to 1, with the payroll clerk earning 548,895 córdobas and the janitor taking home 235,760 córdobas.

Although a hierarchical division of labor existed at the enterprise before the implementation of the SNOTS program, the system institutionalized and codified a new occupational hierarchy. Between 1985 and June 1988, any modifications in this occupational hierarchy, such as incentives and job reclassifications were subject to a complex system of regulations interpreted by the Ministry of Labor. Both workers and management had to submit proposals for job reclassifications and incentive changes to that ministry for its approval or rejection. Moreover, wage and salary increases were unilaterally decreed by the Ministry of Labor during this time period, thus removing fundamental income questions from the bargaining table.

The Incentive System

After establishing the initial stage of the SNOTS system, the Ministry of Labor, in consultation with employers and labor unions, began to elaborate incentive systems for all employees covered by SNOTS: manual workers, proletarianized white-collar workers, professionals, technicians, and managers. Designed to raise productivity and reward efficient workers, these incentive systems were based on the payment-per-results system for manual workers and the payment-per-performance system for white-collar workers, coordinators, and managers.

The Norm System

In addition to defining basic wage and salary scales, the SNOTS program introduced a "norm system" which attempts to establish a daily goal that a manual worker should be able to achieve if he/she works diligently and with little resource waste. Once a norm is established a worker can receive a wage bonus as an incentive for surpassing the norm. At Oscar Turcios both union and management concur that the norm system should be a mechanism to both raise worker productivity and reward workers that surpass productivity goals. But because management's primary objective is to raise productivity and show a profit while the ATC is charged with satisfying workers' basic needs as well as helping to guarantee high worker productivity, conflicts over the norm system have emerged. I will first discuss the difficulties in establishing the norm system at Oscar Turcios and then examine its impact on workers' purchasing power.

The Norm System at Oscar Turcios

In June 1985, the enterprise created a work commission comprising the director, the sub-director of production, the sub-director of work and salary organization, the norm monitor, the head of human resources, the heads of each UPE, union local officials, and the union executive.[24] The work commission's main task was to review established work norms, create norms for as yet non-normed tasks, and approve or modify the proposed worker incentive scheme. The regional tobacco commission, rank-and-file workers, and experienced technicians were assigned to help the work commission evaluate the norm system.

The work commisssion established the first set of norms for Oscar Turcios based on the analysis already prepared by the company's SNOTS commission. The SNOTS commission had monitored work performance in a few dozen job categories on five UPEs and met with workers and union locals to gather their opinions on work norms. The first set of norms was introduced on February 7, 1985, but the enterprise had serious problems monitoring these norms because they were introduced in an unsystematic manner at the height of the harvest season. Moreover, the enterprise had few employees versed in norm implementation and only began to carefully monitor compliance with the system in early April 1985.

In a report published in February 1986, the human resources office acknowledged that key mistakes were made during the introduction of the norm system, often at workers' expense.[25] For example, workers who surpassed the norm occasionally failed to receive their incentive bonuses and some workers who performed two different tasks in the same day—one with a higher piece-rate requirement than the other—were paid for laboring only at the less-remunerated job. At the same time, however, some errors were committed that benefitted the workers. For example, a number of workers were paid a basic wage even when they failed to work a full day or reach the established norm. The office of human resources also noted that UPE supervisors seldom reviewed the norm reports submitted to them by group leaders, and instead issued orders to wage monitors that violated the norm system. Reminding UPE supervisors that norm setting was designed to establish a rational method to measure work output and to distribute wages, the norm report concluded: "One's salary must correspond to one's work—if we fail to understand this principle we lapse into unproductivity, alter the costs of production, and fail to achieve the economic/technical plan, thereby forfeiting economic efficiency."[26]

While management was disappointed with the initial results of the norm system, workers were even more dissatisfied. Given the impression that SNOTS would mean higher wages, most workers experienced no change in their take-home pay. In fact, some groups of workers found they were unable to reach the new work norms. It was not long before high norms became the dominant complaint at union meetings.[27]

Backed by the rank and file, the ATC executive council won a demand for a re-evaluation of work norms in October 1985. In its own report on the norm re-evaluation published in February 1986, the enterprise's norm commission acknowledged that a review of norms had been necessary in order to (1) respond to rank-and-file workers' complaints that many norms were unfair, and to (2) fulfil the enterprise's intention of developing an incentive system to increase worker productivity and to guarantee higher wages to workers who surpassed the established norms.[28]

According to the norm commission report, of the 38 agricultural tasks normed in the 1985–1986 production cycle, 10 were being achieved or surpassed by workers. But while only one norm was considered too low, statistics showed that workers were unable to meet the norms established for 27 activities.[29] The human resources office acknowledged that the norms in most of these jobs had been set too high. In six tasks, however, the administrators insisted that external factors had led to inability to comply with the norm, including technical-organizational deficiencies, workers' failure to complete a full day's work, inadequate equipment, heavy jobs assigned to children rather than adults, and worker indiscipline.[30]

The norm revision for the 1986–1987 production cycle established norms for a total of 54 activities. In 11 activities workers were able to achieve only 26 to 58 percent of the norms; and in 11 other jobs, 62 to 79 percent. On the other hand, workers managed to fulfil 80 to 94 percent of the norms in 18 activities, and completed 95 percent to 123 percent of the norms in 18 other jobs. All told, 62 percent of the workers reached or surpassed the norms during the 1986–87 production cycle.[31] And in the 1987–88 production cycle 84 percent of the workers fulfilled or surpassed their work norms.[32]

Wages, Norms, and Purchasing Power

The most frequent complaint made by enterprise workers concerns the purchasing power of their wages. *"No ajusto con lo que gano"*—"I can't cover my needs with what I earn"—is uttered by scores of workers every payday. Prior to June 1988, workers purchased most of their basic goods from enterprise commissaries. The cost of their purchases was then reduced from their biweekly wage payments. In most cases, these deductions absorbed the workers' entire monthly earnings. Since June 1988, workers have had to pay cash for all goods bought at the commissaries. Since they make their purchases at the beginning of the month—before payday—most workers now borrow money from relatives and friends, promising to pay back the money on payday.[33] A close examination of wages and prices during 1988 shows the extremely limited purchasing power of workers' wages.

As we saw in chapter one, the government decreed a 500 percent wage increase on February 1988 and fixed prices on 46 basic items, called the *canasta basica*. Table 2.2 shows the *canasta basica* with the regulated prices as of February 1988.

In February 1988, the four workers' commissaries at Oscar Turcios offered the following items: sugar, rice, beans, corn, cooking oil, laundry soap, laundry detergent, dish soap, toilet paper, body soap, deodorant, tooth paste, powdered milk, and sanitary napkins. The commissary sold the first eight items on a per-capita basis; that is, workers could buy a fixed amount of each product according to the number of dependents they claimed on their *tarjeta*—purchasing card. The February per capita was 5 pounds of sugar, 5 pounds of beans, 2 pounds of rice, 4 pounds of sugar, 1/4 liter of cooking oil, 1/2 bar of laundry soap, 2 bags of laundry detergent, and 1/2 bar of dish soap. Because of the scarcity and expense of the other items available at the commissary, both workers and management tend to speak of these eight items as *lo basico*—"the basic" products. But at various points during the deepening economic crisis, the ATC has struggled to include other items, such as toilet paper, deodorant, and sanitary napkins, as essential items that the enterprise should provide in modest amounts at subsidized prices.

In February the entire cost of the commissary products—for a worker and five dependents—stood at 675 córdobas, 481 córdobas for the basic eight and 194 córdobas for just two units of each of the six complementary products. At that time most workers on the norm system were classified in levels 3, 4, and 5 in the SNOTS scale, earning between 690 and 900 córdobas a month in base wages. On this extremely low income workers

TABLE 2.2   Prices of Basic Market Basket in February 1988

Product	Price	
Rice (1b.)	4.10	
Beans (1b.)	5.75	
Sugar (1b.)	2.85	
Oil (liter)	12.00	
Salt (1b.)	1.35	
Chicken (1b.)	22.50	
Pork (1b.)	25.00	
Fish (1b.)	22.50	
Pasteurized milk	6.60	
Powdered milk (1b.)	27.90	
Eggs (dozen)	25.00	
Tortilla (1b.)	7.04	
Spaghetti noodles (1b.)	5.65	
Bread (1b.)	10.25	
Pinolillo	5.25	
Ground coffee	25.00	
Laundry soap	5.90	C/U
Detergent	1.25	per bag
Toothpaste	12.70	C/U
Matches	0.60	box of 50
Broom	7.20	
Toilet paper	13.50	per roll
Bath soap	5.10	C/U
Sanitary pads	17.00	per bag
Butane gas	45.00	per 25 1b. tank
Electricity	0.64	KWH
Water	0.80	
Bus tickets	0.50	urban
Deoderant	17.80	
Needles	0.35	
Thread	1.30	
Toothbrush	20.50	

Source: El Machete, February 1988, p. 13.

were able to buy the basic eight but could not afford such essential items as eggs, tortillas, coffee, firewood, or pasteurized milk.

By July 1988 the entire cost of the 14 commissary products had risen to 1,637 córdobas, 628 córdobas for the basic eight and 1,009 córdobas for two units each of the six complementary products. In June workers on the norm system were reclassified three levels in the SNOTS scale and received a 30 percent wage increase, giving them earnings between 1,316 and 1,794 córdobas a month. Thus many workers could no longer buy all the commissary products. What about manual workers who surpassed their job norms? An analysis of two outstanding workers at the main processing facility reveals to what extent incentives linked to the norm system can augment a worker's purchasing power.

During the four-week period from July 5, 1988 to August 1, 1988, one worker, a woman who removes the main stems from cured tobacco leaves, earned 1,859 córdobas.[34] Surpassing her norm by 26 percent, she earned 377 córdobas in incentives. In July, this amount could buy only 3 extra tubes of toothpaste, or 2 extra boxes of sanitary napkins, or 5 rolls of toilet paper. Another woman, the "vanguard" worker in the same job of removing stems, earned 1,987 córdobas in July. Twenty-two percent of her net income, 430 córdobas, came in the form of an incentive for surpassing her norm. Yet with these 430 córdobas this worker could purchase just a few more complementary items at the commissary. Although in July all workers on the norm system received 50–60 percent subsidies on goods purchased at the commissary, it is obvious that the norm-based incentive system failed to add much to workers' wages.

Performance Incentives

While manual workers began receiving incentives linked to the norm system as early as 1985, white-collar workers, coordinators, and managers remained without an incentive system until July 1987. In that month the enterprise introduced an incentive system developed by the Ministry of Labor, a system that had become common in many government offices throughout Nicaragua.[35] The job performance incentive system judges employees according to a fixed number of criteria, assigning percentage values to each of these criteria. Performance evaluations for administrative workers and coordinators are based on five factors: work completion; human relations; labor discipline; judgment; and initiative. Work completion consists of finishing a task on time and with quality. The human relations criterion is defined as treating the public and other workers with "discretion and cooperation." Labor discipline means "fulfiling the supervisor's instructions and meeting the general norms of the institution." Judgment is characterized as the capacity "to think systematically and objectively about any situation that arises in the course of one's work." And initiative comprises the "application of new ideas to improve one's work." In addition to these five criteria, the incentive system measures managers' ability to plan and organize activities as well as their leadership capacity.[36]

Under the job performance system that prevailed between July 1987 and February 1988, each employee was evaluated by his/her supervisor every month and graded according to a complex percentage system: a 96–100 percent rating earned a 60 percent incentive; a 91–95 percent rating earned a 50 percent incentive, an 86–90 percent rating a 40 percent incentive, an 81–85 percent rating a 30 percent incentive; a 76–

80 percent incentive a 20 percent incentive; and a 70–75 percent rating a 10 percent incentive. To receive a 91–95 rating in "judgment," for example, an employee had to meet the following standards:

> [The employee's] performance is more than satisfactory, clearly superior to the majority of workers in his category. His behavior and decisions are mature and logical, generally founded in solid reasoning. He identifies with precision and clarity the problems that arise in his field of work and adopts correct decisions even in relatively complicated situations. He maintains an objective and critical attitude when focussing on job situations and is able to contribute various alternatives in analyzing and resolving work problems. He understands and executes with good judgment the instructions that he receives from his superiors.[37]

Employees welcomed the job performance incentive system, viewing it as an opportunity to increase their incomes. Management, for its part, regarded the system as a way to increase the company's administrative efficiency. During the first months of the sytem's implementation, few employees received ratings high enough to earn 40 percent income bonuses. But by January 1988, the overwhelming majority of employees were receiving incentives of 50 and 60 percent. In the central office, for example, 8 employees received 60 percent bonuses, 21 employees earned 50 percent incentives, and 5 were rewarded with 40 percent bonuses.[38] These figures indicate that by January 1988, with inflation raging beyond control, supervisors and department directors were using the incentive system as a device to help white-collar employees win back some of their lost purchasing power. Indeed, the enterprise director later admitted: "This incentive system clearly helped raise the levels of worker discipline and initiative, but it is true that in the end we tended to give high across-the-board incentives to help resolve workers' wage problems."[39]

Reclassifications

Since the SNOTS program sets income parameters, the ATC has negotiated a number of wage and salary increases by reclassifying job categories. In September 1987, the union convinced management that UPE supervisors, UPE assistant supervisors, and group supervisors should be reclassified according to SNOTS-sanctioned criteria. Prior to this proposal, UPE supervisors were classified in level 14, UPE assistant supervisors were classified in level 8, and group supervisors in level 5. After discussing the union's proposal, the state farm's work commission decided to divide the UPE supervisors and assistant supervisors into two categories and the group leaders into three categories. Taking into account employees' experience in tobacco cultivation, their capacity to lead, plan, and organize work, and their level of literacy, UPE supervisors and assistant supervisors were classified as "A" or "B" in their occupations, while group supervisors were categorized as "A," "B," or "C."[40]

Under this new scheme, an UPE supervisor who was placed in the "A" category jumped from level 14 to level 16 in the SNOTS scale, while an UPE supervisor assigned to the "B" category remained in scale 14. UPE assistant supervisors benefited the most from the new classification scheme. An assistant supervisor ranked in category "A" skipped from level 8 to level 12 and assistant supervisors assigned to the "B" category moved from level 8 to level 10. Group leaders who were placed in category "C" remained in level 5, but those assigned to category "B" transferred to level 6, and "A"-ranked leaders jumped two scales to level 7.[41] In terms of actual wage increases, UPE assistant supervisors in the new "A" category received a 32 percent wage hike, while group leaders who jumped one level in the SNOTS scale gained a 10 percent wage boost. Other reclassified employees enjoyed increases between these two figures.

In May 1988, with the prices of basic goods again rising at an alarming rate, the ATC negotiated a reclassification for all enterprise employees. The measure went into effect on June 6, four months after the implementation of the February reforms.[42] During that period the prices of the *canasta minima*—minimal goods package—rose 634 percent while incomes remained frozen.[43] Although the reclassification won back only a small part of employees' lost purchasing power, it was sweetened by the company's commitment to subsidize half the cost of workers' basic June purchases at the commissaries. As we shall see below, this subsidy served as an important precedent for incentive gains in August 1988.

In the agricultural production sector, in which most company employees work, the reclassifications allowed manual workers to keep pace with the commissary price hikes in complementary goods.[44] All manual workers in normed tasks, for instance, shifted from level 5 in the SNOTS scale to level 8. Some skilled workers, such as tobacco curers, fumigators, and mechanics enjoyed a 4-level jump in the wage scale, while tractor drivers skipped 5 levels. These reclassifications, along with an extremely modest government-decreed 30 percent wage, allowed workers to continue purchasing the basic eight items in the commissary.

Production unit supervisors also benefitted from the reclassifications— their second move upward in less than a year. Group supervisors "A" and "B" transferred from levels 6 to 10 and 7 to 11, respectively, and UPE assistant supervisors "A" and "B" shifted from 10 to 13 and 12 to 15 respectively. UPE supervisors in the "B" category jumped from 14 to 19, while UPE supervisors "A" skipped four levels—from 16 to

20. Credentialled employees in coordinator positions enjoyed similar boosts in the SNOTS scale. Technical supervisors shifted from level 22 to level 26 and the complex director skipped four levels, from 26 to 30. Administrative employees located in levels 14 through 20 moved up 4 or 5 levels, giving these coordinators raises between 30 and 35 percent.

While the reclassification allowed working-class employees to continue buying the basic eight, it permitted most coordinators to augment moderately their purchasing power. The technician that monitors labor resources, for example, jumped from level 14 with a salary of 2,092 córdobas a month, to level 18 with a salary of 2,752 córdobas. She was able to purchase 14 products for herself and 7 dependents. In addition to the 8 basics, she bought 4 rolls of toilet paper, 2 bags of sanitary napkins, 1 bar of body soap, 2 tubes of toothpaste, and 2 one-pound cans of powdered milk. With the special June subsidy provided by the enterprise, she paid only 490 córdobas for a package of goods costing 980 córdobas.[45]

Incentives in Kind

During the month that followed the reclassification, prices of most goods sold at the commissaries surged significantly higher. General service employees were the first group of workers to demand more dramatic reclassifications. After holding an assembly chaired by the service department's union local, the workers drafted an elaborate proposal calling for reclassifications of thirteen job categories. The proposal, directed to the enterprise director, argued that the June reclassification "was not very objective in the service area because none of its employees, not even the department director, participated in its elaboration."[46] The service workers went on to request reclassifications of four to five levels for cooks, gardeners, security guards, a messenger, a janitor, a carpenter, an electrician, the kitchen supervisor, an inventory clerk, a commissary clerk, a construction supervisor, and a security guard supervisor.[47]

The service workers' request for a further reclassification included the following appeal:

At the present time we are seriously affected by the price rise in the basic goods package and in other daily requirements, such as firewood and salt, that are not supplied in the comissary. We therefore appeal to you that the commissary continue to guarantee the sale of deodorant, toothpaste, toilet paper, spoons, sanitary napkins, bath soap, detergent, milk, clothes, and shoes. Without the availability of these goods in the commissary we will continue to fall into the hands of the black market, thereby promoting inflation and speculation.[48]

The service workers made their reclassification appeal at a time when farmworkers in other sectors were demanding incentives in the form of products. In July 1988, for example, cotton workers insisted that their employers guarantee a minimum of eight basic goods to all workers that double their work norm.[49] The director of Oscar Turcios suggested at a consultative council meeting that incentives in kind would be an appropriate way of satisfying the demands of all the enterprise's employees. After a number of work sessions with top management, the union won a package that granted incentives in the form of a graduated system of subsidies for the following products: corn, beans, sugar, rice, cooking oil, laundry soap, dish soap, laundry detergent, and salt.[50] At the time the incentive system went into effect—mid-August 1988—this package of goods was worth 3,958 córdobas for a worker plus four dependents.[51] For the lowest paid workers at the company—those classified in level 6—this represented an incentive of 300 percent more than their base wage.[52]

To receive an incentive, workers on the norm system had to fulfill quality standards in their job, meet their work norm, and measure up to labor discipline requirements.[53] White-collar workers, coordinators, and managers were also evaluated under the new incentive system. But their job evaluations were based on the job performance criteria employed during the period between July 1987 and February 1988. Although workers who had more than four dependents complained that the new incentives would not cover their entire commissary bill, most workers expressed satisfaction with the payments-in-kind plan. For the first time in years they would have an opportunity to earn incentives that would provide the basic eight for free, leaving them with enough cash to purchase some of the complementary goods.

The Social Wage

As we have seen, workers' wage gains have failed to match the skyrocketing inflation rate of recent years. To make up for the steady loss in the monetary income of its members, the ATC has been pressing vigorously for increased social benefits. According to the collective bargaining agreements made with management, these benefits include free food at worksite canteens, commissaries selling basic products, workers' production collectives, occupational health and safety measures, medical attention and medicines, free transportation to and from work, and housing projects.[54]

Workplace Canteens

During the first eight years of the revolutionary process, workers who had no canteens at their work centers were paid a per diem to help cover their lunch costs. This per diem was a benefit that workers won through the ATC's efforts shortly after the revolutionary triumph. Nevertheless, the per diem never matched the actual costs of a lunch, and workers pressed management to build more canteens and provide free food to all workers. This demand received the strong backing of the women's secretariat in the ATC's regional office. In February 1987, the secretariat announced that Oscar Turcios' management had agreed to build eight new canteens on those production units that still lacked cafeterias. Moreover, management pledged to provide lunch—at no cost— at all the canteens on the state farm. By the end of the year management had fulfilled its commitment; eight new canteens had been built, giving Oscar Turcios a total of 14 canteens serving both permanent and temporary employees. In addition to providing free lunches, the company also guarantees breakfast during the harvest to workers who travel long distances to get to work in the morning and dinners to fumigators and tobacco curers who work late hours.

Most lunches at the canteens consist of rice, beans, tortillas, eggs, soup, and a variety of vegetables. Each meal is accompanied by a *refresco*—a fruit or grain drink. Meat is occasionally available. Cooks face the constant challenge of preparing the same foods in different forms in order to provide some measure of variety for workers. As one kitchen supervisor told me: "We try to come up with creative ways of cooking so that workers don't face the same meal day after day."[55] To improve the menu without incurring additional costs, the enterprise has begun to grow vegetables for the canteens and is developing a pig-raising facility.

Workers' Commissaries

The *centros de abastecimiento rurales* (rural supply centers) represent the heart of the social benefit system at Oscar Turcios. The state farm currently runs four worker commissaries that serve both permanent and temporary workers. The advantages that these commissaries hold for workers depend largely on the variety, quantity, and prices of the available goods. In August 1987 the following goods were sold on a per-capita basis to farmworkers and their dependents: rice, corn, salt, cooking oil, laundry soap, powdered milk, spaghetti noodles, body soap, dish soap, laundry detergent, deodorant, sanitary napkins, toilet paper, plastic dishes, diapers, sheets, shirts, underpants, brassiers, shoes, and socks. Since the state farm purchased these goods at wholesale prices from the Ministry

TABLE 2.3   Price Increases of 14 Commissary Products Sold between
February and September 1988

Product	Feb.	Apr.	June	July	Aug.	Sep.
Sugar (1b.)	2.85	2.85	6.15	17.75	31.00	28.25
Rice (1b.)	4.10	4.10	7.40	101.00	75.00	75.00
Beans (1b.)	5.75	5.75	5.75	5.75	50.00	45.00
Corn (1b.)	2.20	2.20	2.20	2.20	8.00	6.00
Oil (liter)	12.00	12.00	12.00	120.00	125.00	120.00
Toilet paper	13.50	13.50	13.50	68.85	121.50	121.50
Dish soap	5.90	5.90	5.90	141.00	141.50	141.20
Laundry soap	5.90	5.90	5.90	67.60	70.00	76.70
Detergent	1.25	3.50	11.00	67.80	67.80	77.75
Bath soap	5.10	5.10	11.00	11.00	--[a]	50.00
Deodorant	17.80	17.80	--[a]	102.73	--[a]	119.00
Toothpaste	12.70	--[a]	13.50	121.00	121.00	121.00
Powdered milk (1b.)	27.90	--[a]	70.00	100.00	295.00	295.00
Sanitary pads	17.00	--[a]	20.00	192.00	73.50	192.00

[a]Unavailable.
Source: Oscar Turcios Chavarria, Department of General Services,
February-September 1988.

of Domestic Commerce the products were sold to workers at prices two
to five times cheaper than in retail outlets.

By August 1988, however, the commissary offered only 15 products—
the basic eight, salt, powdered milk, bath soap, toilet paper, sanitary
napkins, deodorant, and toothpaste. The state farm was forced to cut
the number of products it purchased due to steep price increases in a
number of complementary products. However, the enterprise was still
able to sell the remaining goods at relatively low prices. Since corn and
beans are grown on the state farm, their prices are considerably lower
than those on the free market, and the other 13 items are still purchased
at wholesale prices and resold to workers at cost. Although these goods
are available at cheaper prices than in retail stores, the gap between
commissary and retail prices has diminished sharply since the February
1988 reforms, mainly due to the ending of government subsidies on
complementary items. Table 2.3 shows the effects of inflation on the 15
items sold at the commissary during the 7-month period from February
to September 1988.

Workers' Production Collectives

Every year the ATC negotiates an agreement with the state farm
guaranteeing workers' the right to receive part of the bean and corn
crops grown on enterprise land during the dead season. Magda Espinoza,

who has worked at Oscar Turcios since 1983, explains how this social benefit helped her in 1987:

> This past year my work group planted two *manzanas* of beans. We sold 30 percent of the harvest to the enterprise. Half of the rest of my share I sold on the free market earning the equivalent of two months' wages. I kept the remainder of the beans for my family. The enterprise provides us with irrigation equipment and fertilizers and we do the planting, weeding, and harvesting. It's a good deal for us during the dead season— we keep working on the farm but also have time to cultivate our own crops.[56]

In 1988 the ATC negotiated a somewhat different from of sharing the crop. On most production units workers agreed to deliver to the state farm the first 16 *quintales* of beans yielded per *manazana* and the first 25 *quintales* of corn per *manzana*. All yields above these quotas were kept by the workers. By the end of the harvest—in July—workers had surpassed the quotas, sharing among themselves a total of 23 *manzanas* worth of corn and 21 *manzanas* worth of beans.[57] The state farm sold about half of its share of the harvest, keeping the other half for distribution to workers' canteens and for sale at workers' commissaries. Thus this social benefit provides tangible goods to participating workers while ensuring adequate basic grain supplies at canteens and commissaries for the entire workforce. The production collectives also play a role in increasing the level of basic grain production in the country.

Health and Safety

The leading health hazards in tobacco production at Oscar Turcios stem from pesticides and tobacco dust. Both fumigators and tobacco curers administer pesticides and are subject to the risks involved in handling these chemicals. Moreover, when these workers are careless with pesticides other workers suffer the consequences. In June 1988, for example, seven workers suffered pesticide poisoning at the San Nicolas UPE after drinking water that had been used to clean fumigation equipment. These workers suffered dizziness, sweats, trembling, and nausea. Fortunately, their exposure was limited and their symptoms were only temporary. However, fumigators and tobacco curers, who are exposed daily to pesticides, risk more serious health problems. Diseases affecting the nervous system and cancer are only two of the long-term consequences of prolonged exposure to pesticide chemicals.

Men and women who handle cured tobacco in the processing facilities constantly inhale tobacco dust. Many of these workers suffer frequent headaches and respiratory problems. Prolonged inhalation of tobacco dust can lead to brown lung. During the 1985–1988 period, three women at the Jose Ortiz processing facility retired on disability as a result of contracting this disease.[58]

Since 1985, the ATC, working with the enterprise's health and safety department, has implemented a series of measures to address the health hazards inherent to tobacco production. Before each planting season, the health and safety technician conducts seminars for fumigators, tobacco curers, and warehouse workers, explaining the correct handling of both pesticide containers and fumigation equipment. Furthermore, all workers who handle pesticides are given blood tests every two months to determine the level of pesticides in their bodies. Workers whose blood tests show a high level of pesticides are immediately offered jobs that involve no further chemical exposure. At the same time, the health and safety department has acquired masks for all workers who classify tobacco in the pre-industrial facilities. Unfortunately, very few workers have chosen to wear these masks, complaining that it aggravates their headaches.[59]

The health and safety department has also fought for measures limiting the amount of time that certain workers spend in curing rooms where the air is the most difficult to breathe. During 1986 and 1987, the enterprise submitted a number of formal requests to the Ministry of Labor asking for permission to allow these workers to work only four hours a day in curing rooms and four hours a day in another location. But the ministry consistently denied this request. Consequently, in October 1987, the enterprise informed the ministry that they were reducing these workers' workday to six hours due to their adverse working conditions.[60]

Medical Attention and Medicines

Since 1986 the health and safety department has arranged regular medical check-ups for enterprise employees. These check-ups are available at a medical post located behind the state farm's main pre-industrial facility. The enterprise also maintains a supply of medicines and first-aid kits at each production unit. In addition to consultations provided by a general practitioner, eight to ten medical specialists visit the enterprise once a month to examine between 100 and 150 workers. Each month a different group of workers receives these consultations. When necessary, the specialists refer workers suffering from chronic problems to doctors in health centers and hospitals in the area. In such cases the state farm covers the worker's medical expenses.[61]

Housing

The ATC is also fighting for low-cost housing to help attract new workers to the state farm and benefit veteran workers and single mothers with many children. In 1986 the ATC signed an agreement with the National Construction Union of Finland to build a 50-unit housing project at Isidrillo, a village located near four of Oscar Turcios' production units. Upon their arrival in November of that year, the Finns insisted on working with Nicaraguan workers because, as brigade leader Jukka Numminen explained, "We wanted to exchange experiences and teach them new work methods."[62] Together, they completed the houses in record time and went on to build ten more. Encouraged by its success, the union began a second stage of the project in May 1987. A year later, they had completed the outbuildings and were busy installing the showers, toilets, laundry tubs, plumbing, and drainage ditches. In addition to the 50 houses, the Isidrillo project will include an elementary school and child-care center. The ATC is promoting another community housing project at Arenal, one of the four UPEs located just south of Condega. In 1984 Arenal's workers began to press management to fund new housing in order to stabilize and augment their unit's labor force. In 1986 workers borrowed money from management to build four houses and in 1987 solidarity groups in the United States began a fundraising campaign to support the construction of eight more houses. On January 3, 1988, some eighty contras attacked both Arenal and the German Pomares agricultural cooperative located just above the Arenal housing project. In the aftermath of the attack the cooperative members asked to be relocated at the Arenal housing site. The ATC accepted their request and the farmers began building four houses in February. The project thus became a joint farmworker-campesino community, and a new governing council made up of workers and farmers renamed the project after a Sandinista martyr, Jose Benito Jiminez.

The Jiminez community project also includes the construction of a three-unit elementary school that will serve 150 students. The first unit was inaugurated in March 1988, and the second and third units will open in 1989. The ATC has also solicited funds for two more aspects of the project—a bridge and a child-care center. A river that separates the community from the Pan-American highway is too deep for vehicles to cross during much of the rainy season. The ATC would like to construct a durable concrete bridge across the river. The child care center would relieve the domestic burden of many of the mothers who work at Arenal and the other three state farm units adjacent to it.

Both the Isidrillo and Jiminez community projects have faced a myriad of problems. The most crucial difficulty centers on financing the construction costs. Since the money is donated in dollars, the sharp fluctuations in exchange rates during 1987 and 1988 has sometimes adversely affected the purchasing power of the donations. For example, from February until June 1988, the dollar was drastically undervalued. During this period the government converted a large sum of dollars donated by the Finns into córdobas. A sudden currency change devalued the córdobas and the donation could no longer cover the cost of building a water tank for the project. Consequently, in June, the state farm assumed 80 percent of the construction costs for the water tank. At the same time, a 50 percent loss in the value of dollars designated to buy equipment and furniture for the project's child care center has postponed the inauguration date of that facility.[63] And at the Jiminez community, the ATC's reliance on foreign donations has caused intermittent delays in implementing the project.

Authority Relations

Since the triumph of the revolution authority relations within state enterprises have changed drastically. Under Somoza workers were given orders by supervisors which they would never think of questioning. Relations between workers and most supervisors were marked by hostility and mistrust. The anti-Castro Cubans who ran the tobacco farm had the power to punish and fire workers and never hesitated to use or abuse that authority. And the workers—unorganized and intimidated— had no means of redress. Nohelia Gutierrez, a worker with 19 years of experience in tobacco production, emphasizes the differences for women workers before the revolutionary triumph and after:

Under Somoza we worked in the tobacco fields like beasts of burden. I remember being pregnant a couple of years before the revolution. I worked until my labor pains became unbearable. I didn't dare ask to leave the fields until then—they would have fired me. Today if a woman doesn't feel well in the morning, she rolls over in bed and goes back to sleep. And today we women get three months paid pregnancy leave. Imagine that! That's one of the many reasons I will always work for the union. And why I will always work for the revolution.[64]

Traditional authority patterns were ruptured with the triumph of the revolution. Workers, newly-affiliated with the Rural Workers Association and fresh from their triumph over the National Guard, were in no mood to accept their former position as humiliated subordinates. In addition to demanding decent wages and work conditions, they insisted on being treated with dignity by supervisors, production unit heads, and enterprise management. The most noticeable consequence in the workers' new attitude was a sharp fall in productivity. After working at hard, pain-staking, and even hazardous work for years to make profits for owners, the revolutionary triumph gave them the opportunity to realize a concrete benefit—less work.

> During the 1980 production cycle, the state farms employed more persons per unit of land, yet produced less value than the private capitalist farms. This falling productivity could not all be attributed to the additional number of workers given year-round employment. Perhaps even more significant was the fact that on many publicly owned farms, the average work day in practice has dropped from seven to about five hours or even less. When workers were paid to do a set piece of work, they finished as soon as possible, with quality often suffering.[65]

In June 1988, during a worker/management council meeting, the head of the main processing facility presented a report on the quality of the 1987–88 tobacco harvest. Only one third of the cured tobacco leaves were of export quality—a precipitous drop from the pre-revolution era and a significant drop over 1984, the best year in terms of quality since the triumph. After his presentation, an intense discussion ensued, with supervisors and technicians complaining that the damage to the leaves caused by workers was largely due to the undisciplined behavior of workers who failed to carefully handle the tobacco. But most workers who participated in the debates—as well as some supervisors—blamed the fall in quality on the norm system which rewards workers according to the amount of tobacco they sew onto curing poles, untie from the curing poles, classify according to type, and so on. Or, put another way, since the norm system is based on payment per *quantitative* results rather than *qualitative* results, workers hasten to fulfil and surpass their norm, damaging tobacco leaves in the process.

Despite the differences between workers and supervisors over the cause of the fall in tobacco quality, all participants agreed that all of the enterprise's employees were suffering the results; the enterprise had less quality leaves to export each year, and, since wages and incentives were now to be based primarily on a company's profit margins, both wage workers and salaried employees would be adversely affected.

The debate on how to overcome the problem of poor quality tobacco continued during the weeks that followed the extended council meeting. During one impromptu meeting between workers and UPE supervisors held in the main classification facility in July, 1988, the UPE heads insisted that authority relations had to change during the cutting, threading, and post-curing phases of the production process. Quality control, they argued, needed to become a priority with supervisors scrupulously checking workers' handling of the tobacco leaves to make sure they were not tearing or squeezing the leaves. One UPE supervisor after complaining that he and other supervisors received resentful replies from workers whenever they criticized poor quality work, suggested that the ATC assign one experienced worker to assist supervisors in quality control: "With a respected union leader participating in checking workers' output we can avoid both mistreatment of workers on the part of supervisors and resentment of supervisors on the part of workers. But as it is now, our authority is not respected."[66]

At the same time, the ATC's secretary of labor and social affairs, insisted that workers had to be paid based on the quality of their work. If pay is based largely according to the careful handling of the tobacco leaves rather than the amount of leaves processed, she contended, workers would not rush to surpass norms and less leaves would be mishandled.[67]

This entire debate on quality control points to a fundamental contradiction that exists in Nicaragua's state sector. While the pre-revolutionary hierarchical relations between workers and supervisors has been ruptured, providing an unquestioned benefit for workers, both productivity and quality have fallen, harming the standard of living of workers as well as other popular sectors. Yet this contradiction seems inherent to a revolutionary process, especially in a country as undeveloped economically as Nicaragua.

Worker Participation on the State Farm

As Carole Pateman points out, true worker participation in management "involves a modification, to a greater or lesser degree, of the orthodox authority structure; namely one where decision making is the 'prerogative' of management, in which workers play no part."[68] Many writers on management use the term "participation" to refer not just to a method of decision making, but also to cover techniques used to persuade employees to accept decisions that have *already* been made by management. This type of situation is *pseudo participation*. Pseudo-participation occurs, for example, when a supervisor, instead of merely announcing a decision, allows workers to question him/her about it and discuss it.

Genuine participation in management, however, involves participation in decision making itself. Moreover, there are two fundamental types of participation: "partial participation" and "full participation." Partial participation occurs when workers affect the decisions of management but management retains the power to make the final decision. Full participation takes place when each individual member of a decision-making body has equal power to determine the outcome of decisions. Moreover, partial participation and full participation can exist at both "lower" and "higher" levels of management. The lower level refers broadly to those management decisions relating to control of day-to-day shop floor activity, while the higher level refers to decisions on such matters as investment and marketing.[69]

In Nicaragua rural workers face formidable obstacles in their efforts to participate in economic management. As Austin and Ickis explain:

> Workers in Nicaragua were accustomed to either an adversarial relationship with management or a submissive role, making it difficult for them to adopt a problem-solving orientation from the perspective of the total enterprise. They have empirical knowledge and skills related to production processes, but their lack of formal education and their previous isolation from management decision-making may cause them to neglect areas such as finance or commercialization.[70]

At Oscar Turcios workers and their representatives mainly participate in lower-level economic decision-making. The bulk of this decision-making occurs in the three consultative forums that exist on the state farm. The first, base-level consultative body is the *production council*, an organism that functions on each of the 14 production units. The production council comprises the UPE supervisor, the UPE technical supervisor, the various group leaders, and the member of the union local. Production council members are charged with reviewing the progress of the UPE's technical/economic plan, resolving any problems that arise in the plan's implementation. The second decision-making body is the *amplified council*, an institution that operates on each of the state farm's four complexes. The complex director, UPE supervisors, group leaders, and union local secretary-generals, as well as top management attend amplified councils to discuss advances and obstacles in the production process at the complex level. Wages and incentives are also debated at these forums. The highest decision-making body on the enterprise is the *consultative council* made up of the director, departmental directors, and the union executive's general secretary. Union local officials sometimes attend consultative council meetings and the ATC often sends a regional secretary to participate in the discussion. "Higher-level" management decisions are made at such meetings, giving union delegates a direct voice in executive decision-making.

Forrest D. Colburn, in his book *Post Revolutionary Nicaragua*, asserts that Nicaraguan workers are not concerned with participation:

> Surprisingly, the lack of worker participation does not seem to be a major issue among laborers, who seem much more interested in having adequate management than in playing a role in it. Worker complaints about man-

agement seem to center on the lack of technically capable administrators, and not on the absence of a role for themselves.[71]

Yet many workers at Oscar Turcios take a considerable interest in worker participation. According to Olga Maria Talavera, a union leader at the main processing facility,

> It is untrue that workers do not want to participate in decision making. We do have the desire and the right to participate based on our knowledge of the enterprise's situation. Under Somoza we only worked for our wages but now many of us are very interested in understanding the economic situation of the enterprise. Knowing how much is produced and the profits that the enterprise earns provides us with the financial information we need in order to make our demands.[72]

Nowhere have the state farm's workers had a greater impact on decision making than in matters related to the norm system. Indeed, worker participation in the norm system has eliminated much of the exploitation that plagues workers paid by piece rates in other countries.

Worker Participation in the Norm System

Many labor analysts argue that the piece-rate system is inherently exploitative of workers. Summarizing the history of the piece-rate system in the U.S. apparel industry, Louise Lamphere writes:

> Given the low-profit, labor-intensive, and highly competitive nature of the industry, the apparel manufacturer has always sought to get as much work out of the workers as possible. The piece-rate system has been the main method of keeping production high. The piece-rate system had its beginning in the "task-system" of the 1870's. A team made up of a machine sewer, a baster, and a finisher was paid by the "task," until it became difficult to complete even four or five tasks a week. Early strikes attempted to abolish the task and contracting systems, and to substitute a weekly wage. In 1919–1920 the three major unions were able to establish weekly wages in their major contracts. Some contracts retained piecework, however, and a "log" or schedule system replaced the old task system. Each type of garment was divided into working parts with rates fixed on each part. During the 1920s the unions lost the battle to eliminate piecework, since an expanding number of small, nonunion shops paid piece rates and severely threatened the unionized sectors of the industry. The unions were willing to accept responsibility for establishing "standards of production" for those workers paid on a weekly basis, but they were never able to convince management that the workers would produce a "commensurate"

amount of work under weekly pay. By the mid-1930s the return to piecework was virtually total.

Although the piece rate is now a fixture of every garment shop, worker suspicion of management's use of piece rates has persisted. Women sewers, like their predecessors in the early period of unionization, feel that the system can be used against them. They realize that it induces individuals to "speed up," which causes fatigue, promotes individualism rather than collectivism among the workers, can be used to shorten the season since it encourages workers to get the work out faster and earlier, and by setting times by the faster workers can be used to cut rates, hence lowering the wage.[73]

Moreover, as Michael Burawoy details in the case of the Red Star factory in Hungary, the piece-rate system can be used to subjugate workers under socialism as well as under capitalism. Burawoy explicitly blames the piece-rate sytem at Red Star for the intense wage insecurity suffered by the workers there:

How was it that workers cooperated in their own barbaric subordination? The need to survive and the power this gave to management were obviously critical. Yet there was something about the labour process that generated a certain complicity of the workers in their own subordination. The mechanism through which workers were drawn into their own dehuman- ization was the uncertainty of outcomes. "Insecurity is the main driving force in all payment by results. . . . The manifest coercion and dependence which characterize payment by the hour change into a semblance of independence with piecerates. . . . Uncertainty is the great magician of piece-work."[74]

It is my contention, however, that the piece-rate system need not be inherently exploitative of workers. An analysis of the norm system at the Oscar Turcios state farm reveals four principal reasons why the piece-rate or norm system is not an inherently oppressive production apparatus. First of all, workers and their union representatives at Oscar Turcios participate directly in the setting and revision of norms— management cannot unilaterally establish nor alter a norm. Unlike Red Star, where the foreman dictated the norms without any consultation whatsoever with the workers, workers at Oscar Turcios contribute to the norm setting process. Moreover, as we described above, rank-and-file workers were consulted during the original studies conducted by the Oscar Turcios SNOTS commission in 1984. And when most of the 1984–85 norms proved to be unattainable, a large number of them were lowered as a result of worker pressure.

A second reason that the norm system is not inherently oppressive at Oscar Turcios is that norms are set according to rational calculation, not personal whim. The human resources office's division of work organization and salaries collects data on worker output and calculates in minute detail the percentages of workers who fall short of the norm, reach the norm, and surpass the norm. The work division also calculates the average rate of norm completion. And the enterprise administration can propose an increase in a norm only if the average rate of fulfilment is more than 130 percent.[75] Moreover, the administration must submit any norm revision proposals to the regional norm commission for its review. A representative of the ATC sits on this commission and can argue the union's case against management in this forum. According to ATC officials, the union seldom loses a battle over norm-setting. Julian Salinas, ATC secretary of production at the enterprise level, recalls one case won by the union:

> In late 1986, the enterprise proposed that the norm for pesticide fumigators be changed from one *manzana* per day to fourteen hundred-weights of tobacco equals 1.8 *manzanas*, an area that even our most efficient fumigators cannot spray in one day. I made the case for maintaining the norm at one *manzana* and the commission rejected management's proposal.[76]

Thus, at Oscar Turcios differences over norms are resolved through the application of rules, in which the decisive production apparatus is the regional norm commission. And the ATC has a key voice on this commission. At Red Star, however, norms were set according to the arbitrary will of the foreman:

> So everyone is dependent personally on the head foreman who fixes the level of his pay: this is a paradox of piece-rates. The only concern one worker has for the others is jealous suspicion. Are the others a few fillers (unit of currency) ahead? Is their hourly rate going up more quickly? Are they getting more of the best "good" jobs that are going? Such rivalry is equally fierce over all matters in which the head foreman's decision is final: holidays, overtime, bonuses, awards.[77]

A third reason why the norm system does not oppress the workers at Oscar Turcios is that the norms are established according to the capacity of workers with average abilities—that is, the norm system is designed to meet the needs of what one union leader calls *el obrero regular*, "the average worker":

We in the ATC must fight for the average worker. The union strives to guarantee a fair norm for workers who don't have tremendous productive capacity. And the majority of the average workers are reaching or surpassing the norms in tobacco jobs. In a revolutionary country the norm system must be used as a tool to regulate work in a way that allows workers of modest abilities to maintain themselves. So in Nicaragua the norm system is not a method of exploitation but rather a mechanism that permits workers to earn according to their genuine capacities.[78]

In most piece-rate systems workers have no recourse if management fails to provide the conditions necessary to reach a norm. At the Allied machine factory in Chicago, for example, Burawoy reports that workers "became angry with management when it failed to provide the necessary conditions—acceptable piece rates, adequate tooling and fixtures, prompt service from auxilary workers, and so on—for making out."[79] At Oscar Turcios, however, workers are entitled to receive their normed wage if the enterprise fails to provide the conditions necessary to fulfil a norm. An ATC union official explains: "If a worker who sews together pieces of cheesecloth (used to cover tobacco plants) runs out of thread and the enterprise is unable to resupply him, management must pay his wage at a hundred percent of the norm."[80] Thus, providing workers with the necessary conditions for meeting norms represents the fourth reason why the piece-rate system at Oscar Turcios fails to oppress the workers.

It is the arbitrary aspect of most piece-rate systems that leads to worker oppression. Moreover, arbitrary aspects of the norm system also engender divisions among workes. At the Red Star factory, where looting is the key to earning a decent wage and its possibility is limited, operators are reluctant to share their accumulated experience. New operators confronted this when they arrived on the shop floor to be trained by a senior operator who ran a similar machine. If the apprentice was willing to play along with the instructor by producing a large number of pieces to augnment the latter's earnings, then he might learn something. But he would not be taught the tricks that made looting possible, nor the adapted fixtures that turned a bad job into a good one. Such angles the new operator had to learn for himself by closely observing others, or elicit by trading favors.

(The instructor) doesn't let me work on both machines at once, although I'm going to have to do this eventually. He sets up one machine so quickly that I can hardly see how he goes abut it, and then he leaves me to put a run through. Meanwhile, he's milling on the other machine himself, and he doesn't utter a single word until I've finished. There's a hint of blackmail in his way of going about things: if I agree to play along, perhaps he'll agree to explain the odd thing to me, now and then. From time to time, he knocks off early and asks me to punch his card for him. In exchange, he's quite prepared to spend half an hour telling me how things work.[81]

At Oscar Turcios, on the other hand, where looting is not required to reach the norm, new workers receive the full support of more experienced workers. For example, I have observed tobacco threaders with five or more years of experience patiently teach new threaders how to efficiently sew tobacco leaves onto curing poles. Moreover, these veteran threaders forfeit some of their own earnings during the hours spent instructing the novices. In this particular job threaders are given an eight-day probation period during which they are guaranteed the standard wage for threaders. And if during the first six days after the probation period a woman is unable to at least earn the minimum agricultural wage she is given the option of working at another job where she can earn at least the minimum.

Class relations on the state farm are marked by both conflict and cooperation. The wage question, especially acute in Nicaragua as a result of hyper-inflation, engenders continual struggles among the enterprise's three social groups as each attempts to maintain its standard of living. Through constant bargaining with management the state farm's workers have obtained a package of social benefits that was out of reach under the Somoza dictatorship and still unobtainable in the private sector. Authority relations have also been transformed on Oscar Turcios. No longer subjected to abuse on the part of dictatorial bosses, workers toil in an atmosphere that allows them to challenge and reject authoritarian behavior on the part of supervisors and management. Even more, despite formidable obstacles, workers have taken the first steps toward worker participation in management. In sum, the revolution has begun to fulfil its goal of making a more acceptable use of national resources in the interests of the working class.

Notes

1. Wright, *Classes*, p. 151.
2. Oscar Turcios Chavarria, "Ficha Ocupacional: Responsable de Produccion Agricola."
3. Ibid.
4. Oscar Turcios Chavarria, "Ficha Ocupacional: Responsable de Recursos Humanos."
5. Ibid.
6. Wright, *Classes*, p. 151.
7. Oscar Turcios Chavarria, "Ficha Ocupacional: Responsable de Programa."
8. Ibid.
9. Wright, *Classes*, p. 151.

10. Ibid.

11. Oscar Turcios Chavarria, "Ficha Ocupacional: Tecnico de Complejo y Selección de Semilla."

12. "Central administration" includes the central office, the transportation department, one canteen, and a workers' commissary.

13. Oscar Turcios Chavarria, "Ficha Ocupacional: Tecnico "C" en Recursos Laborales."

14. Ibid.

15. Oscar Turcios Chavarria, "Ficha Ocupacional: Responsable de Expendios."

16. Ibid.

17. Oscar Turcios Chavarria, "Ficha Ocupacional: Segundo Responsable de UPE."

18. Ibid.

19. I discuss the norm system later in this chapter.

20. Material on the implementation of the SNOTS system is drawn from a report issued by the enterprise's human resources department, *Evaluación General: Normas de Trabajo y Salarios,"* February 21, 1986, pp. 2–8.

21. This figure represents workers' total net income: base income, overtime, and incentives.

22. Tractor drivers earned between 7 and 27 percent of their total net wages in overtime.

23. This figure represents coordinators' total net income: base salary and incentives. Coordinators are not paid overtime.

24. This section draws on Oscar Turcios Chavarria, *Evaluación General: Normas de Trabajo y Salarios*, February 21, 1986.

25. Ibid., p. 4.

26. Ibid., p. 5.

27. Interview with Eligio Castellano, enterprise health and safety technician, June, 1986.

28. Oscar Turcios Chavarria, *Evaluación General: Normas de Trabajo y Salarios*, p. 10.

29. Ibid., pp. 10–11.

30. Ibid., p. 10.

31. Oscar Turcios Chavarria, Deparment of Human Resources, *Recuperación de los Rendimientos y La Jornada Laboral en el Campo*, January 26, 1987, pp. 5–6.

32. Oscar Turcios Chavarria, *Informe Evaluativo Ciclo 87–88, Avance Ciclo 88–89*, July 6, 1988, p. 18.

33. In August I interviewed 30 workers in levels 7 and 8 in the SNOTS scale. Twenty-six told me they borrowed sums ranging from 500 to 2,000 córdobas to buy the basic eight goods in July. The other four were granted credit to purchase their goods, agreeing to pay back the company on their next two paydays.

34. These earnings and subsequent amounts in this paragraph were taken from the processing facility's payroll report, July 5, 1987 to August 1, 1988.

35. See Ministry of Labor, *Resolución del Ministerio de Trabajo Relativa al Pago por Eficiencia en el Desempeño del Cargo,* 1986.

36. Oscar Turcios Chavarria, *Evaluación del Desempeño,* 1987.

37. Ministry of Labor, *Resolución del Ministerio de Trabajo Relativo al Pago por Eficiencia en el Desempeño del Cargo,* p. 9. The Ministry of Labor's standards for awarding an "excellent" rating to an employee are remarkable. To receive a 96– 100 percent rating in labor discipline, for example, an employee had to meet the following standards: "The employee is exemplary in his personal conduct and fufills exactly the instructions of his hierarchical superiors as well as the norms that regulate the work of the institution. He takes maximum advantage of the workday. He never arrives late. He rarely fails to come to work, and when absent always has a justifiable excuse. His tardiness occurs at most twice a month and accounts for less than an hour per month. He makes personal telephone calls only in cases of emergency and they are always brief and concise" (ibid., p. 7).

38. Oscar Turcios Chavarria, *Planilla de Administración,* December 12, 1987 to January 20, 1988.

39. Interview with Hector Valdivia, enterprise director, August 1988.

40. Oscar Turcios Chavarria, *Memorandum: Ubicación de Categorias y Salarios,* November 17, 1987.

41. Ibid.

42. Oscar Turcios Chavarria, *Memorandum: Promoción de Escala Salarial,"* July 4, 1988.

43. Instituto Historico Centroamericano, "Las Medidas de Junio: Paquete Sin Pueblo," *Envio,* (July-August, 1988), p. 15.

44. The prices of the six principal complementary products rose 35 percent between February and June.

45. Interview with Berta Rugama, labor resources technician, August, 1988.

46. Memorandum from general services personnel to Director Hector Valdivia, July 25, 1988. The union executive board was also unhappy with the reclassification, claiming it was not implemented according to the original agreement between the ATC and management. (Interview with Julian Salinas, SUE secretary general, August, 1988.)

47. Ibid.

48. Ibid.

49. *Barricada,* July 17, 1988.

50. Oscar Turcios Chavarria, *Reglamento de Incentivos a traves del Abastecimiento a todos los Trabajadores de la Empresa,* August 15, 1988, p. 13.

51. Ibid., p. 1.

52. Ibid., p. 19.

53. Ibid., p. 2.

54. See Oscar Turcios Chavarria, *Convenio de Producción Ciclo 88–89,* March 23, 1988.

55. Interview with Nohelia Gutierrez, kitchen superviser at UPE Villa Vieja, July 1988.

56. Interview with Magda Espinoza, manual worker, August 1987.

57. Interview with Alberto Martinez, ATC secretary of organization Region I, August 1988.

58. Interview with Eligio Castellano, enterprise health and safety technician, July 1988.

59. Ibid.

60. Oscar Turcios Chavarria, *Memorandum: Ubicación de Categorias y Salarios*, November 17, 1987.

61. Interview with Eligio Castellano, enterprise health and safety technician, July 1988.

62. *Barricada Internacional*, "Finnish union builds commitment," June 30, 1988, p. 10.

63. Oscar Turcios Chavarria, *Entrega de Viviendas del Proyecto de Viviendas Isidrillo*, June 22, 1988.

64. Interview with Nohelia Gutierrez, group leader, October 1987.

65. Joseph Collins, *What Difference Could a Revolution Make?*, p. 74.

66. Taken from my notes at the meeting, July 1988.

67. Ibid.

68. Carole Pateman, *Participation and Democratic Theory* (Cambridge: Cambridge University Press, 1970), p. 68.

69. Ibid., p. 70.

70. James E. Austin and John C. Ickis, "Management, Managers, and Revolution," *World Development* Vol. 14, No. 7, p. 776.

71. Forrest D. Colburn, *Post Revolutionary Nicaragua: State, Class, and the Dilemmas of Agrarian Policy* (Berkeley and Los Angeles: University of California Press,), p. 118.

72. Interview with Olga Maria Talavera, ATC secretary of production in main processing facility, September 1988

73. Louise Lamphere, "Fighting the Piece-Rate System: New Dimensions of an Old Struggle in the Apparel Industry," in Andrew Zimbalist, ed., *Case Studies on the Labor Process*. New York: Monthly Review Press, 1979, p. 260.

74. Michael Burawoy, *The Politics of Production*, (London: Verson, 1985), p. 169.

75. Interview with Marietta Paz, director of human resources, January 1988.

76. Interview with Julian Salinas, SUE secretary of production, January 1988.

77. Quoted in Burawoy, *The Politics of Production*, pp. 173–174.

78. Interview with Julian Salinas, January 1988.

79. Burawoy, *The Politics of Production*, p. 173.

80. Interview with Eligio Castellano, enterprise health and safety technician, January 1988.

81. Quoted in Burawoy, *The Politics of Production*, p. 174.

Women workers uprooting young tobacco plants to be transplanted in the state farm's UPEs

Author (at right) and friend with ATC secretary of production

Workers moving irrigation hoses at UPE, La Joya

Close-up of worker kneeling to uproot baby tobacco plants

Worker transplanting tobacco plants in freshly irrigated row

Young worker displaying handful of young tobacco plants

Piece-rate monitor weighing a box of tobacco ready to be classified

Women workers performing laborious task of classifying tobacco leaves

Gender Relations

3
A key element in the unprecedented participation of women in the Nicaraguan revolution is their role as "pillars of their families."[1] This is the basic reality of life for Nicaraguan women. They don't view themselves merely as housewives caring for their children, attending to domestic concerns, and subordinating themselves to their husbands. Women are the center of their family—emotionally, ideologically, and economically. This is especially true of working-class and peasant women.

Single mothers abandoned by their husbands constitute 34 percent of urban households in Nicaragua.[2] Even when husbands remain with their families, the high rate of both seasonal and permanent unemployment among men places the burden of family survival on women. This daily struggle to survive is responsible for strong, well-developed, and determined personalities among Nicaraguan women.

The participation of women in the war against Somoza strengthened their character even further, and precipitated many changes in their views on traditional gender roles. AMPRONAC, the organization that mobilized women against the dictatorship, offered its members a crucial vehicle for participation by encouraging women to break from their prescribed roles to become politically active anti-Somocistas. For many women, political activism led to conflicts within the home, even separation from husbands and children. Indeed many women engaged in a double clandestinity: hiding their political involvement from their husbands and the National Guard. But as men began to recognize the important role that women were playing, they came to treat women with new respect.

Gloria Carrión, one of the founders of AMPRONAC, describes the effect that women's political involvement had on relationships between men and women:

> Women began to develop their own points of view on issues and began to express their ideas. In homes where both the husband and wife lived together new relationships developed. Women started to make their feelings and opinions known. They would disagreee with their husbands on issues

75

where they never had before. And as women got involved in activities outside the home their time was less fully devoted to the home and the division of labour within the family began to change. All this demanded a re-evaluation of the family situation.[3]

Participation in the struggle against Somoza also brought a sense of self-respect to many women. One domestic worker who had raised nine children alone declared: "Women weren't aware of anything; they only washed, ironed, cooked, had children and that was it. But now, I tell you, we're awakened."[4]

Even in revolutionary movements, however, there is no guarantee that participation will lead to a permanent political role in the new society, or that it signifies a genuine step toward emancipation. History has many examples of societies in which women participated in social and political conflicts only to be forced back into traditional roles when the crises subsided.[5]

Although thousands of women developed a feminist consciousness during the revolutionary war, sexism still thrives in Nicaragua. The battle to end the oppression of women is an arduous and protracted one that is only just beginning. Women still maintain primary responsibility for child-rearing and housework; initial attempts to liberate women from such traditional tasks face immense obstacles. In addition, transforming patriarchal ideology and behavior—challenging men to change relationships from which they have gained definite privileges—is a difficult task in any society. In the post-revolutionary era, it has fallen to the Nicaraguan Women's Association, AMNLAE, to tackle the country's heritage of deep-rooted sexism.

AMNLAE's Position on Women's Liberation

For AMNLAE getting women into waged work and out of the home is a key step toward their liberation. Waged work gives women economic independence, the organization argues, and this makes them equal to men. It also brings them into what AMNLAE sees as the "public," and thus, the political arena. In this respect, then, the women's organization agrees with the orthodox Marxist-Leninist position on women which attributes the origins of women's subordination to their marginalization from "productive" work. AMNLAE echoed this view in an important 1980 article:

At a given moment in the history of the social division of labor, women were separated from production and assigned to domestic labor. With this assignment the world of women was reduced to the atrophying dimensions of the home, to a narrow framework that was limited and individualist. In addition, they were subjected to exhausting and routinized work. This gradually generated in women a political, technical, and social backwardness which converted them into objects propelled by history, not subjects forging their own history.[6]

The FSLN, to which AMNLAE is closely affiliated, contends that full equality for women—their complete integration into society—can only arise through the consolidation of the revolution:

> In Nicaragua, women's interests are promoted principally through the defense and consolidation of the Revolution. The defense of the Revolution will be strengthened with new female contingents of combatants, workers, teachers, professionals, etc., as we eliminate any obstacles which impede women's integration or maintain discrimination. The struggle to wipe out discrimination against women cannot be separated from the struggle to defend the Revolution, which is the fundamental task of our entire people at this moment in history. The massive incorporation of women in all the tasks of the revolution is necessary for the maintenance of popular power and the building of a new society.[7]

This "integrationist" approach is fundamental to AMNLAE's strategy for working women. The women's association views work as a first step toward women's emancipation, and dedicates itself to encouraging women to work outside the home. Consequently, AMNLAE is committed to policies that free women from household tasks. The association calls for the socialization of housework and helps establish day-care facilities. The scarcity of resources and the escalating contra war, however, have severely limited such projects.

Although AMNLAE champions women's role in production outside the home, few association leaders or activists hold to the orthodox Marxist-Leninist view that women's path to emancipation is assured *solely* by participation in the work force outside the home. Rather, many AMNLAE members call for a revolution in patriarchal patterns of thought and action. One association activist summarizes the views of her sisters:

> We have a great responsibility to push for a change in values. We have to overcome the current situation and make the family a joint responsibility. Children have to receive values from fathers as well as mothers; the formation of a new society is a responsibility of both parents. . . . The patriarchal system is much more difficult to overcome [than capitalism] because patriarchy exists also between men and women who love each other and live together.[8]

Thus AMNLAE's "integrationist" policies are tempered by its emphasis on the importance of developing new relations between women and men, and the creation of a new ideology that will help liberate women from age-old oppression.

Nicaraguan Women and Employment

In Nicaragua women have worked outside the home in large numbers for many generations. Indeed, Nicaraguan women's intense participation in the revolution is largely attributable to their notable participation in the economy. As Margaret Randall writes:

> Nicaraguan women have been continually pushed beyond the narrow domestic scene. While the Spanish Catholic tradition preached of women in the home, passive, dependent and "ornamental," the world around them demanded something else. History forced them to assume positions and make decisions which, along with their economic activity, increased their social and political involvement.[9]

Unfortunately, few statistics are available on Nicaraguan women's economic participation. In 1950, women comprised 14 percent of the economically active population (EAP). By 1970 this figure had risen to 21.9 percent and in 1977 it was 28.6 percent. More recent figures reveal that women comprise 40 percent of the urban EAP.[10] Because more than half of the population lives in urban areas, and domestic labor—which still employs many women—is not included in the statistics, this figure provides only a partial analysis of the situation. There is no similar data for rural areas. It is estimated that women make up about 35 percent of the total—urban and rural EAP.[11]

In Latin America as a whole, women comprise only 20 percent of the labor force. Thus the percentage of Nicaraguan women working outside the home is remarkably high. Nevertheless, during the early years of the revolution Sandinista leaders complained that relatively few women were involved in "productive" work. For example, in a 1982 speech celebrating AMNLAE's fifth anniversary, Interior Minister Tomás Borge asserted: "If we analyze the type of work women carry out, we see that a high percentage of these women are really under-employed, and that another large layer is employed in domestic service—work that is not productive and that will have to be regulated and limited in the future."[12]

Of all women who work outside the home some 20 percent work in agriculture, 20 percent in personal services, and 20 percent as market or street vendors.[13] The overwhelming majority of women living in towns—78 percent—work in commerce or services. In Managua, women represent 70 percent of the domestic service workers and 55 percent of the merchants. But women comprise only 14 percent of Managua's industrial labor force. Most women work not to provide a second income, but rather to maintain the home as the sole wage earner. According to some estimates, 83 percent of working women are heads of households. The figures for Managua indicate that women head 49 percent of the families and of these women 85 percent are economically active.[14]

The Feminization of the Rural Labor Force

As in most Latin American countries, rural women in Nicaragua have been economically marginalized and doubly exploited: as peasant farmers or farmworkers, and as women. Various studies of rural women in Latin America indicate that conventional figures underestimate women's role in the rural economy. For example, these studies identify the male head of the household on small farms as the principal agricultural producer and therefore economically active. The women and children are considered non-paid family assistants and are counted as economically active only if agriculture is their principal activity. As a result, investments, and social benefits are skewed to address the role of men in the economy.

Even when rural women do not work the land, many of them raise animals, process agricultural products, or perform other agricultural tasks. Before the revolution, studies ignored such activities and sharply underestimated the number of women in the rural labor force. Nicaraguan government studies since 1979 demonstrate that women have participated significantly in the rural labor force. During the most intense period of the contra war, between 1983 and 1986, thousands of rural women entered the rural work force, supplanting men who were mobilized to fight the war. Some officials estimate that women now represent 75 percent of the coffee pickers, and 60 percent of the work force in cotton and tobacco.[15]

Indeed, since 1983 a feminization of the agricultural labor force has been occurring in Nicaragua. This feminization process includes three aspects. First, due in large part to the contra war, thousands of women have been entering the rural work force and now represent a large percentage of the total rural proletariat. Second, women are increasingly engaged in agricultural tasks that once were the exclusive preserve of men, thus partially rupturing the sexual division of labor in the countryside. Third, more and more women are engaged in productive activity year round or at least six months a year—that is, a growing percentage of the female labor force in agriculture are becoming permanent workers.[16]

While this feminization of the agricultural proletariat has occurred in all the principal export crops, it is particularly marked in tobacco. Thus, in Region I, where Oscar Turcios is located, 76 percent of the permanent workers and 63 percent of the temporary workers were women during the 1984–85 production cycle. In fact, of the total number of tobacco workers in Region I that year, men represented only 25 percent, while women comprised 55 percent. Children made up the remaining 20 percent of the workforce.[17]

The ATC and Women Farmworkers

Despite the high participation of women in agricultural work, the ATC failed to adequately address women farmworkers' concerns during the revolution's first four years. It was only after strong pressure from below that the ATC finally convened a conference to address the situation of female workers in April 1983. Held in the city of Granada, the meeting focused on their political, organizational, labor, and social problems.[18]

Women's family responsibilities, delegates complained, prevented them from participating fully in the life of their union. They also criticized their husbands for failing to understand their desire to be involved in union activities. Many of the women explained that union leadership positions were beyond their grasp as long as they remained barely literate. Women who care for children could not attend adult education classes because the classes were held at night. Furthermore, some delegates accused two state farms of failing to grant women equal pay for equal work, a practice contrary to Nicaraguan law. Other delegates reported cases of discrimination in hiring and training, and instances where women were prevented from joining the union. Finally, conference participants reported that some pregnant women miscarried during the coffee harvest because they had been assigned to work on difficult terrain.

Delegates offered suggestions to overcome these problems, including an educational campaign to inform women of their rights and a proposal to guarantee women access to technical training courses. The ATC studied and debated the concerns raised at the conference, and adopted measures to address some of them. One regional office decided to guarantee 20 percent of its leadership positions to women, and to hold training courses for women or with women comprising a majority of students.[19] In the meantime, women at all levels of the ATC began to apply pressure to gain equal rights in the union.

In 1984, the national office of the ATC established a women's secretariat designed to formulate policies centering on women farmworkers' concerns. Since its founding, the secretariat has fought to increase social benefits for women workers, to strengthen women's participation in training programs, and to challenge the gender-based division of labor on private and state farms. Women now sit on each of the ATC's national commissions as well as each of the association's regional offices. And in 1987 AMNLAE, the Nicaragua Women's Association, began assigning women activists to help ATC union locals promote women's struggles in farms throughout the country.

In September 1986 women farmworkers held their second national assembly. The main goals of the assembly were to assess the progress made since the first assembly and set an agenda for future work. After several days of intense discussions the assembly developed eight working resolutions that have guided the association's recent work on women farmworkers' issues.

1. We will continue fulfilling the accords reached at the Second Balance of the National Union Assembly "Leonel Rugama."
2. We will increase our integration into all modes of defense as well as increase our moral and material support for those mobilized in the Patriotic Military Service.
3. We will guarantee our active mobilization in the harvests, both in the labors of cutting and in support work, and we will integrate more women into cultivation work. This is a decisive factor if we are to emerge victorious from the present harvest cycle and to prepare ourselves for the 1987–88 cycle.
4. We will meet and surpass the norms, producing the maximum with the few resources at our disposal. Where we confront difficulties we will participate in a creative and combative manner to improve work organization. We will demand that management adhere to the descriptions and technical characteristics of each normed job.
5. We will include in our plans of struggle and collective bargaining agreements . . . the installation of day care facilities, children's cafeterias, electricity, running water, collective laundry areas, and corn grinders. We will also demand other social benefits, such as maternity subsidies and full pay for workdays lost due to a child's illness.
6. To contribute to the self-sufficiency of our sector, we will sponsor more union and company gardens, particularly in the private sector. We will struggle so that the Ministry of Domestic Commerce guarantees us more regular supplies of underwear, dishes, shoes, medicines, machetes, radios, and other goods at reasonable prices.
7. We will intensify our participation in adult education and struggle for more spaces for women in technical and union training. We

will seek union backing to overcome the obstacles preventing us from participating in such activities.

8. We will guarantee that all of the union structures include these resolutions in their plans and evaluations. To achieve this objective in union locals, we will integrate more women into union leadership positions and include vanguard women workers in union councils.[20]

In September 1987, after a series of base and regional assemblies involving more than 7,000 women, the ATC held its third national assembly of women farmworkers. During this assembly delegates analyzed their gains and problems in the areas of defense, production, social benefits, and political-ideological work. While renewing their commitment to increasing the country's production of agroexports and foodstuffs, the women also urged their union locals to struggle for the fulfillment of contractual clauses that benefit women workers. These clauses include the construction of child-care centers and dining halls, the provision of health and safety equipment, and the guarantee that women be fully paid during maternity leaves.[21]

Clearly women farmworkers in Nicaragua have set themselves a challenging agenda. An examination of their situation at the national level as well as at the Oscar Turcios enterprise reveals that women agricultural workers have made some important gains but that much more remains to be done. We begin by analyzing a problem that affects women everywhere—the sexual division of labor.

The Gender Division of Labor

The division of labor concept appears in Marx's own work almost as often as the class concept, and he uses both in an equally ambiguous and equivocal fashion. In *The German Ideology* Marx employs the division of labor category in a broader and more fundamental manner than that of class.[22] Indeed, Marx asserts that the division of labor accounts for specific differences and contradictions within a class.[23] The division of labor concept designates a set of phenomena both broader and more concrete than that of class. The concept refers specifically to the *activity* of labor itself, and the particular social and institutional relations of that activity, rather than to a relation to the means of production and the products of labor, as does class.[24] The specific location of individuals in the division of labor explains their consciousness and behavior, as well as the concrete relations of cooperation and conflict they experience.[25]

Because the division of labor concept is more concrete in its level of analysis and broader in scope than the category of class, it is a crucial tool in any analysis of social relations involved in and arising from laboring activity. As Iris Young elaborates:

> Each category entails a different level of abstraction. Class analysis aims to get a vision of a system of production as a whole, and thus asks about the broadest social divisions of ownership, control, and the appropriation of surplus product. At such a level of abstraction, however, much pertaining to the relations of production and the material bases of domination remains hidden. Division of labor analysis proceeds at the more concrete level of particular relations of interaction and interdependence in a society which differentiates it into a complex network. It describes the major structural divisions among the members of a society according to their position in laboring activity, and assesses the effect of these divisions on the functioning of the economy, the relations of domination, political and ideological structures.[26]

In capitalist society the division of labor is not essentially a division of tasks but rather the separation between their conception and execution, and the establishment of management, hierarchy, control and differentiation of functions. Inherent to the capitalist division of labor in large-scale industry is the development of specialized technical and managerial functions, supervision, the establishment of specialized departments such as tool-room, maintenance, quality control, and production, and also the creation of a hierarchical ordering by skill within them.[27]

This technical division of labor, however, is not the only division of labor inherent to capitalism. The gender division of labor is intrinsic to the capitalist division of labor as a whole, and pervades every part of it. It exists in all industries and it takes both a vertical form—women generally located at the bottom of any job hierarchy—and also a horizontal one, with women and men occupying very unevenly different functions and work categories.

Of course, the gender division of labor is not limited to the industrial sphere. It exists in the domestic realm as well. Indeed, as we saw in the case of Christine Delphy, many feminists argue that the gender division of labor originates in the domestic sphere, where women have traditionally provided domestic services and child-rearing services for men. We therefore turn to what feminists often call women's domestic burden.

The Burden of Domestic Labor

In capitalist and socialist societies, women assume most of the burden of domestic labor, while men assume most of the responsibility for the provision of commodities. This division of labor between women and men, which is accompanied by a system of male supremacy, originates as a historical legacy from oppressive divisions of labor in earlier class societies. The particular separation between domestic and wage labor generated by the capitalist mode of production then strengthens this division of labor. Domestic labor increasingly occurs in specialized social units—most often the family—whose isolation in space and time from wage labor is further accentuated by male domination. These conditions mark domestic labor with its specific qualities.[28]

The particular nature of domestic labor under capitalism engenders strong feelings of opposition between one's private life and the public sphere. As Lise Vogel, a leading Marxist feminist, elaborates:

> The highly institutionalized demarcation of domestic labor from wage labor in a context of male supremacy forms the basis for a series of powerful ideological structures, which develop a forceful life of their own. Isolation of the units of domestic labor appears to be a natural separation of women from men as well. Confinement to a world that is walled off from capitalist production seems to be woman's time-honored natural setting. A series of correlated opposites embodies the seemingly universal division of life into two spheres of experience: private and public, domestic and social, family and work, women and men. Rooted in the economic workings of the capitalist mode of production, and reinforced by a system of male supremacy, this ideology of separate spheres has a force that is extremely diffficult to transcend. Where some categories of male workers command wages sufficient to maintain a private household staffed by a nonworking wife, the ideology takes a particularly stubborn institutional form.[29]

The ideology of separate spheres remains deep-rooted in Nicaragua. Very few people question the belief that domestic work is the exclusive task of women. And studies confirm that nearly every household duty is carried out by women. The 1984–85 joint study shows that women heads of household performed 58 percent of all domestic jobs without the help of other members of the family.[30] They alone cooked, washed clothes, ironed, hauled water, went shopping, and brought their children to health centers. The study indicates that a daughter performed 14 percent of the domestic tasks, while the rest of the work was carried out by the single mother with the help of other women.[31] Married women carry the heavy burden of the double shift as well, performing 53 percent of the household tasks unaided. Daughters and mothers of married women do the other domestic jobs.[32]

At the same time, male participation in domestic work is negligible. The 1984–85 study indicates that husbands, brothers, and sons performed, at most, six percent of the household tasks and these were primarily jobs considered "masculine," such as securing firewood for the family.[33] The majority of the women interviewed in the study felt that men should share household tasks. One woman worker asserted: "The man has to participate in something at home. Housework is not only the woman's problem."[34] Nevertheless, one third of those women who think that men should share domestic work saw no possibility of that happening.[35] This sentiment was summed up in the words of one woman: "It would be good if the men helped but they don't like it and they don't do it."[36] Only 17 percent of the women workers interviewed disagreed with the idea of shared housework.[37] The view of these women was expressed in the following remark: "Men are for other types of work; the house is for the woman."[38]

Like their sisters throughout Nicaragua, women workers at Oscar Turcios suffer the effects of the double shift. The overwhelming majority of women on the tobacco farm are single mothers. According to a survey I made in August 1988, of 238 women with children working at the enterprise's main processing facility and six production units, 166 women— 70 percent—were single heads of households.[39] And many of these women had no extended family members or older daughters to help with domestic chores. Indeed, of one group of 20 women that I interviewed, 12 said they performed all household jobs alone. At the time of the interviews, these women were working a 7–5 shift, returning home by 6.00 p.m. Most worked until 10 or 11 at night and all day Sunday to keep their homes in order. There is no doubt that the energy expended to perform domestic chores saps women's strength to produce adequately at the workplace. Indeed, constant fatigue is one of the women's most common health complaints.

To be sure, women workers at Oscar Turcios do not only face the burden of housework. For inextricably linked to their domestic work is their responsibility of mothering. The overwhelming majority of women workers at Oscar Turcios are mothers. All but 25 of the 238 women in my study were mothers, and the mothers had an average of 3.5 children. The most obvious burden of mothering is the time commitment. With little or no assistance, most of the mothers cook breakfast and dinner for their children and do all their laundry. Moreover, 73 percent of the mothers have at least one child 6 years old or younger and these younger children require frequent medical attention. As a result, many mothers who work on the state farm spend several days a month taking their children to local health clinics. Taking time off to seek medical care for children often means less pay for these women, since most of them are on the norm system. As a result, one of the major demands raised by participants during the 1987 women workers' assemblies was for health care availability on the state farm.

In addition to attending to their children's material and physical needs, the mothers—like all mothers—attempt to meet their children's psychological needs for nurturance and affection. This aspect of what Ferguson and Folbre call "sex-affective production" is the most difficult and vexing problem for the women at Oscar Turcios. For the physical demands of their manual work at the enterprise as well as in the home leave them too little energy and time to adequately fulfill their children's emotional needs. As one mother of 12 young children told me: "I have so little time to pay attention to my young ones. It makes me sad to think how much affection they are wanting and how little I can give." Immersed in their struggle for survival, the women at Oscar Turcios must neglect many of their children's needs—not to mention their own.

At least some mothers at Oscar Turcios have received aid in easing one of the many burdens entailed in the "double shift." In 1984 Oscar Turcios inaugurated its first child-care center—the Los Laureles Center for Rural Infant Services—built with funds provided jointly by the Ministry of Social Security and Social Welfare (INSSBI) and management. The center attends to 97 children and maintains a staff of 20 women. In June 1988 INSSBI began construction on two additional rooms for the Los Laureles facility. These rooms will allow the child-care center to accomodate more pre-schoolers (3–5 years of age.) In 1987–1988 another child care center designed to accommodate 120 children was built at the Isidrillo community project by the Denmark-based World University Service. But because of problems in obtaining electrical supplies and furniture, this center will not begin operating until 1989.

These two child-care centers, however, will not meet all the child-care needs of women workers at Oscar Turcios. Extrapolating data from my 1988 study, the 440 mothers at the enterprise have approximately 685 children of child-care age—more than three times the number of children that the two child-care centers can handle. The ATC is currently soliciting funds for a third child care center for women who work at the four production units in the Condega area.

Many women whose children have attended the Los Laureles child-care center lament the lack of a child care facility for children over the age of six. As one mother comments: "The children who leave the center after completing their pre-school years at the SIR are accustomed to having child care. When they begin primary school and come home in the afternoon they feel lost." Some women who have no other adults in the home to take care of school-age children prefer not to send their children to school. Afraid that a son or daughter may get into trouble without adult supervision before and after school, these mothers also support the demand for a center for school-age children. Many mothers have suggested that such a center provide vocational training for teenagers, employing skilled workers from the state farm. Child-care workers at Los Laureles have backed the demand for a children's center, offering their own voluntary labor to help build such a facility.

In her 1976 essay on marriage and divorce, Christine Delphy observed: "When there are children, the responsibility for their care continues to be borne exclusively by the woman after divorce, and this burden is increased by the financial cost."[40] At Oscar Turcios 70 percent of the women workers are single mothers abandoned by the fathers of their children. In nearly every case these single mothers are heads of households, solely responsible for the expenses involved in their children's upbringing. Working mainly in jobs with very low wages, these women are often unable to afford such basic items as clothing. Indeed, many of their children go to school barefoot. Although the enterprise occasionally obtains children's clothes and shoes for sale at the commissary, the amounts are limited. The ATC sometimes acquires donations of clothes, selling them to workers at nominal prices with the proceeds used to finance union activities.

Mothers of school-age children must also pay for certain expenses related to their children's studies. In August 1988, for example, women had to rent school books for 100 córdobas a year and buy notebooks, pens, and pencils costing another 330 córdobas a year. And because the education ministry lacks sufficient funds, many mothers are asked to contribute money for events at school such as parties and graduation ceremonies. At some schools mothers are even asked to contribute to the cost of paying security guards.

Thus the responsibilities of maintaining their homes and caring for their children weigh heavily on the women who work at Oscar Turcios. Like their peers throughout Nicaragua, women on the tobacco farm remain shackled by their domestic burden. As the joint study concludes:

Women's proletarianization in agriculture entails a double workload: their domestic work and their work as agricultural workers. The fundamental effect is the reinforcement of their subordination because, despite the break with the sexual division of work in the production sphere, the hierarchical man/woman relationship has not changed in the reproductive realm. The fatigue and deterioration of these women is intensified by their double workload. The gender division of labor in the reproductive realm limits the incorporation of women into production in equal conditions with men and will continue to do so as long as measures are not taken to resolve the contradiction that exists between the socialization of the productive sphere and the privatization of the reproductive sphere.[41]

The Gender Division of Labor at the Workplace

The first fundamental aspect of the division of labor is between conception and execution: between those who plan and control activities and those who carry them out. In Nicaragua, as elsewhere, such activities are largely reserved for men. At Oscar Turcios men occupy 40 of the 65 coordinator and managerial posts and in technical jobs there are 20 men employed for every woman.[42] In supervisory jobs, too, the ratio of men to women is high, about three to one. However, the focus of this section is on other aspects of the division of labor by gender: in particular the division between men and women in working-class jobs. The form this takes in Nicaraguan agriculture can best be seen by showing how male and female workers were distributed into different jobs at Oscar Turcios during the height of the 1987–1988 harvest cycle.

Oscar Turcios employed 1,600 manual workers in its 14 production units during January 1988.[43] According to a study I conducted in four of those UPES that month, the division of labor between male and female workers ran among three overlapping lines.[44] First, certain functions in the production process were monopolized by men. There were no women workers operating or servicing tractors, working in the curing process, providing security, or fumigating tobacco plants, and very few women worked as supervisors of work teams in the cutting, threading, and hoisting processes. Eighty-two percent of female working class employees were found in production, with the remainder in such activities as quality control, piece-rate monitors, warehousing, and canteen work. The male workers, on the other hand, were found in almost all the functions in the production units, with the result that only 52 percent of the male working-class employees were found in production jobs. Second, even when women and men were to be found in the same areas of activity—in production, mainly—they were often situated in different jobs. Male and female workers rarely performed the same activities with the same job titles.

The third aspect of the gender division of labor concerns wages and skill. In January 1988, the enterprise had a large variety of occupational titles—more than 50 for manual workers. These occupations were grouped into 13 levels on the SNOTS scale, each associated with a fixed wage. The highest paid manual workers in the enterprise could earn up to three times as much as the lowest-paid. The male monopoly of tractor driver and maintenance jobs meant that there were many more men in higher-grade occupations than women. And the male workers were spread across seven levels more or less evenly while women workers were concentrated at the bottom: none had jobs higher than the tenth level, and 98 percent of them were in jobs in the bottom three (levels

3–5). In fact, the vast majority of women production workers—79 percent of those in production jobs and 72 percent in all working-class positions— were classified in level three, the lowest-paid occupation in the enterprise (excluding children). In other words, men were spread across a wide variety of occupations, while women were concentrated in a few low-paid occupations at the bottom of the job hierarchy.

One major reason why the gender division of labor is so sharply skewed at Oscar Turcios is the continued prevalence of patriarchal ideology in Nicaragua. We thus turn to the ideological beliefs that fuel the gender division of labor.

Ideological Factors that Impinge upon the Gender Division of Labor at the Workplace

The joint study conducted in 1984–1985 found that supervisors and male union leaders depicted women workers as having the following characteristics: soft, rapid in manual work, flexible, physically weak, obedient, submissive, fearful, and without leadership qualities.[45] In contrast they described men as rough, tough, physically strong, capable of leadership, and knowledgeable in all the various jobs of each crop's production cycle. While they regarded women's tasks as soft, light, simple, manual, and not dangerous, they considered men's jobs to be heavy, dangerous, and more complex. For example, these men felt that the most important obstacle to women's participation in traditionally male activities in cotton was their lack of training. And men with supervisory positions on coffee and tobacco farms argued that women lacked the physicial strength to perform the strenuous jobs that men carried out.

But, as the joint study authors argue, a closer analysis of the division between male and female jobs shows that many of the requirements for jobs historically held by men are training and experience—not physical force. This is especially the case in those activities involving supervision and work organization: supervisors, administrators, group leaders, task counters, planners, and tractor drivers. And in technical occupations, such as fumigators and entomology lab technicians, avoiding health risks involves knowledge of occupation health procedures, not physical ability.

At the same time, the study's authors point to the hypocrisy of the argument that claims men's jobs "are too heavy for women," noting that many women workers carry weighty loads of firewood to their homes which are often kilometers away. Moreover, many female jobs that men consider to be light and without danger involve considerable burdens and risks. Fertilizing the soil in coffee production, for example, involves carrying 50-pound sacks of fertilizer.

Behind the dual and sexist division of labor, according to the study's researchers, lies a hierarchical separation of primary (masculine) and secondary (feminine) work forces. Those in the primary work force occupy jobs and positions that tend to be year-round and higher paid. These tasks also require training, experience, and skill, and carry considerable prestige due to their importance. The secondary labor force is concentrated in temporary jobs with low pay, little prestige, and that require an exhausting amount of effort. Moreover, these jobs sometimes involve repulsive aspects that only women and children perform, such as worm removal in tobacco.

At the same time, however, the shortage of male labor power has led to a break in the strict gender division of labor within Nicaragua's rural work force. Since 1983 the entire notion of female and male jobs, light and heavy work, has been subject to intense questioning. This rupture in the hierarchical structuring of the labor force—which began in the war zones—has partially transformed the hiring attitudes of supervisors and administrators. At the same time, the rupture has helped women workers discover and develop new work skills, thereby breaking the patterns of subordinated work to which they were accustomed. While they have not reached the masculine norm, in others, such as coffee processing, they are surpassing the males.

Again, women in war zones who have worked in a number of once male-only jobs are prepared to move into others as soon as they receive the training. "This shows us," the researchers comment, "that equal opportunities must be given to women workers to assume any task and that they should not be limited by a false protectionism. And this does not mean that we neglect necessary work safety requirements, only that an excessive protectionism must not be converted into discrimination."[46]

It is interesting to note that the break in the gender division of labor among rural workers first occured in so-called heavy and dangerous manual activities and only later in management and supervisory positions. Though these occupations do not require physical strength and do not endanger health, in 65 percent of the farms studied women held none of these posts. Twenty-five percent of the supervisors interviewed on these farms—mainly coffee enterprises—asserted that women lacked the necessary qualities for such positions since they were indecisive, informal, incapable of gaining respect, and lacked courage. Another 22 percent of the supervisors—largely on cotton plantions—argued that women lacked training for administrative jobs due to their low level of education, lack of expertise, and inexperience. Tobacco supervisors expressed the view that there was no need for women in management jobs since they were already filled by men, mainly permanent workers with many years of experience.

Despite the sexist ideology held by these supervisors, the researchers noted that the contra war was opening a breach in male conceptions concerning the division of labor:

> The war situation punctures the ideological obstacles that limit women within the productive sphere and sustain the gender division of labor. This is clearly shown by the fact that women are increasingly performing heavy or dangerous work activities. . . . The best way to eliminate the gender inequalities at the workplace is to have a mix of both women and men in all jobs, including those regarded as feminine. Then those jobs that require dexterity, carefulness, and concentration will no longer be considered "feminine" tasks that only warrant minimum wages.[47]

Year-Round Employment

Aurora Gonzales, who has worked 11 years in the tobacco industry, comments on one of the most important recent advances made by women tobacco workers—year-round employment:

> At the time of the triumph of the revolution we only got work in the harvests. There was almost no work for women in the dead season. But since 1984 we have been entering new jobs. In tobacco, for example, we participate in all of the cultivation jobs. That means that today many of us work almost all year round. But still there are many administrative and technical positions that we women can fill.[48]

Under Somoza, very few women were employed year-round in tobacco. Nearly all the female workers were hired to plant seeds and thread tobacco leaves onto curing poles. Once they had completed these jobs the women were fired. Now at Oscar Turcios 200 women and girls lower curing poles from rafters and separate the leaves from the poles during the dead season, jobs that were previously restricted to male workers. Women also pack tobacco in boxes for shipment abroad, another task once held only by men. Moreover, more and more women are entering supervisory positions within the production units, positions with year-round responsibilities and decent salaries.

Women Workers and the Norm System

Threading cut tobacco requires considerable dexterity, quickness, and stamina. A threader uses a sharp, eight-inch needle to sew together pairs of tobacco leaves onto wooden poles. She must jab the needle through the stems of two leaves and then pull the leaves through the string until they are attached to the pole. During the 1986–87 production cycle, the norm for threaders was 140 poles a day. Because the work is performed standing up and requires constant arm and shoulder movements, a threader's greatest output occurs in the morning. By afternoon the threaders' shoulders and upper backs ache. To gain more time to surpass the norm, most women work straight through their one-hour lunch breaks, preferring to eat at their work stations.

During the month of February 1987, I monitored the productivity of 26 threaders in the Villa Vieja production unit.[49] Eight threaders were between 30 and 40 years old, 15 threaders were in their twenties, and 3 threaders were teenagers. Most of the older women threaders worked seven months a year in the main processing facility as tobacco classifiers, while a number of the younger women were temporary workers. During the four-week period of my study, only 6 of the 26 women managed to thread more than the norm of 140 poles. Five of these six women were veteran threaders in their thirties. The "vanguard" worker, 32-year-old Pastora Castillo, threaded an average of 253 poles during February, 81 poles more than the second-most productive threader.

During the 1986–87 harvest season workers received a 50 percent bonus for each unit of work that surpassed their work norm. Thus tobacco threaders, who were paid 4.5 córdobas for each pole threaded up to the norm, earned an additional 6.75 córdobas for each threaded pole after 140. But the actual incentive earnings did not amount to much in actual purchasing power. Pastora Castillo, for all her efforts in February 1987—surpassing the norm by an average rate of 79 percent a day—only earned 22 percent above the basic wage for threaders. Nevertheless, all those threaders that surpassed the norm by at least 50 percent a day during the 1986–87 tobacco harvest earned more than the UPE group leaders whose work is not normed.

Union Participation and Training

In a path-breaking book published by the ATC in 1985, *Revolution and Rural Women*, the section on rural women workers' participation in decision-making begins:

> Women workers are not directly present in decision-making bodies in the state sector. They have a minimal participation in union local executive committees because they confront serious obstacles in incorporating themselves in union life. The double shift—involving domestic and extra-domestic work—requires a 14 to 16 hour workday which leaves women with no time for union activities and no time for rest. Their high number of pregnancies consumes their energies and obligates women to dedicate a large part of their time and energy to pregnancy, breast-feeding, and

child care. Her condition as a temporary wage worker, who returns to the status of *maintained wife* or to the informal sector, objectively limits the development of her class-consciousness. Women workers don't attend union assemblies, not only because women are making dinner for their children at that hour, but also because they don't feel that discussing the goals of the technical/economic plan or a crop's production process relate to their concerns as women.

Diverse ideological factors serve to reinforce women workers' lack of motivation. On the one hand, the predominant social view is that attending meetings, speaking in assemblies, or discussing productivity with management are not *women's concerns*. On the other, the lack of experience in self-organization is greater among women while their educational level is lower than among men. And women have still not overcome their lack of self-confidence. At the same time, the fear of speaking in public is aggravated when such participation means raising concerns related to women's conditions that lack the collective recognition that class issues receive.[50]

The concerns expressed in this passage, especially the need for women to obtain leadership posts in the union, were first addressed at the 1983 women farmworkers assembly. But little was done at that time to improve the situation. By 1984, women comprised more than 30 percent of the ATC's membership, but the number of women in union leadership positions was minuscule. At Oscar Turcios, only 15 percent of the union local leaders were women in 1984, at a time when women made up more than 40 percent of the farms' permanent labor force.

In 1985 the ATC began a concerted effort to increase the percentage of women in union leadership positions. During the 1986–1987 harvest season more than 50 percent of the union local leaders at Oscar Turcios were women—triple the 1984 number. Nationally, as of September 1986, 177 women were leaders of union locals and 20 women were secretary-generals of enterprise unions.

The presence of more women in union posts has been a major gain for female farmworkers. While significantly more women now lead union locals, many of them lack the skills to be effective advocates for the rank-and-file. Why is this the case? Nicaraguan unions, including the Rural Workers Association, suffer from a series of interrelated problems. At the center of these problems is the shortage of experienced union organizers. Each local is supposed to have five secretaties: a secretary-general, and secretaries of organization, health and safety, production, and labor issues. But most locals function with only three or four secretaries.

At Oscar Turcios, the ATC maintains 19 union locals, but in August 1987 only 12 of them had their full complement of union officials. The

shortfall is largely due to the heavy responsibilities and sacrifices associated with union leadership; union officials must attend meetings,
often forfeiting bonus incentives as a result of organizing activites
conducted during work hours, and receive no pay for their union activities.
Consequently, few workers run for leadership positions and a high rate
of turnover exists within union locals.

Moreover, the new people elected to replace burnt-out officials often
plunge into their work without any idea of how to proceed. Their
ignorance is largely due to the union's inability to provide ongoing
leadership training, an inability that stems from too few material resources
and too little time. For example, at the beginning of the 1986–87 harvest
season, the secretary-general of the union council uniting all the locals
at the Oscar Turcios state farm was planning a series of classes for the
dozens of newly-elected officials. But he and his colleagues were swamped
with work during the harvest, attending to the introduction of a new
norm system and emergency problems such as labor shortages. In
addition, many union officials were working overtime and simply lacked
the energy to attend classes. The educational scheme never got off the
ground.

ATC leaders are keenly aware of the need to provide training for
union leaders, especially their new women cadres. A recent concern has
been the problem of poor communication between union local officials
and the rank-and-file, particularly the failure of representatives to consult
the rank-and-file after union council meetings (which involve only union
leaders). This communication failure is largely due to the low educational
level of union leaders, and, once again, the union's lack of resources.
Some union leaders have no experience in taking notes at meetings,
and those who do often have no access to pens and notebooks. In
August 1987, the ATC carried out a number of seminars designed to
teach union representatives how to effectively conduct their tasks. Seminar
participants also received free notebooks and pens to use at future
meetings. Significantly, the money for these seminars and materials was
donated by solidarity groups in the U.S.

Despite the obstacles to women tobacco workers' participation in
union affairs, the Rural Workers Association has introduced measures
to upgrade their involvement in the life of union locals. Indeed, as early
as 1985, the ATC national office recognized the progress made by the
tobacco sector in this realm:

> We must acknowledge the exceptional situation in the northern tobacco-
> producing zone of the country where a massive number of women and
> children work in nearly all cultivating jobs, and where counterrevolutionary
> aggression has been felt since 1982. There, the initiative of the FSLN and
> the ATC to incorporate women workers in all levels of the union structure

means that the war has precipitated the organization and militancy of women in tobacco. These workers have used their leadership positions to make both class and gender demands, at least to a greater extent than women workers in cotton and coffee.[51]

Women Workers' Assemblies

At Oscar Turcios the ATC has promoted women workers' participation in union activity in a number of ways, the most important of which is women workers' assemblies. An outgrowth of the ATC's second national assembly for women workers in September 1986, women workers' assemblies at the enterprise have played a crucial role in augmenting rank-and-file participation in union life. These meetings, exclusive to women, resemble the consciousness-raising groups that arose during the initial stages of the women's liberation movement in the United States and Europe. Although exclusive to women, Melania Castillo, the union executive's secretary of social and labor affairs, invited me to attend a half-day assembly held at the main processing facility on August 15, 1988. The following is an account of that meeting.

At 1:00 p.m. about 150 women gathered at the canteen adjacent to the processing facility. A zonal official of the Nicaraguan Women's Association opened the assembly, announcing the schedule for the afternoon. The main part of the assembly was devoted to small group discussions of the resolutions drawn up at the third assembly of women farmworkers and AMNLAE's "plan of struggle." The women who attended the group discussion chaired by Melania Castillo began by complaining that they were unfamiliar with the resolutions document they were charged with reviewing. The ATC official reminded them that she and others had read the resolutions to all the women at the processing facility in November 1987, six weeks after the assembly was held in Managua. But she acknowledged that insufficient follow-up discussions had taken place since November.

Castillo then proceeded to read the resolutions pausing after each one to elicit reactions from the group members. Although most of the women felt that they had fulfiled most of the goals outlined in the resolutions relating to increasing worker productivity and discipline, nearly all of them felt little progress had been made on some of the resolutions concerning women's issues. Resolution four, for example, calls for action on collective bargaining clauses that require management to provide such benefits as collective laundry and corn-milling facilities. Yet management at Oscar Turcios had made no efforts to provide these facilities. And the women criticized management for ending its subsidies of construction materials for home improvements, another element of the contract agreement. The group participants were also critical of the lack of sex education and family planning seminars, a demand raised in resolution six. Castillo said the union had to take the blame for failing to plan such seminars with the Ministry of Health.

The group discussion ended with a litany of complaints about the supply situation at workers' commissaries. Women pointed out the limited amount of goods they can buy with their earnings. Some observed that certain items, such as powdered milk, should be part of the minimum package, while others bewailed the high prices of complementary products. Indeed, low wages and high prices dominate conversations among women workers whenever they gather to discuss collectively their situation.

The assembly ended with a plenary session in which representatives from each discussion group read the notes taken during the caucuses. A heated discussion broke out during the plenary session concerning the lack of communication between a group of 16 women who received special health seminars a month before the assembly and then failed to subsequently share their knowledge with their sister workers. At the end of the plenary session, the AMNLAE representative read the names of women who would represent the other workers at the regional women's assembly scheduled for September. Union leaders at the processing facility chose the delegates based on their level of participation during the small group meetings. The plenary session ended at 5:00 p.m.

Women workers at Oscar Turcios are engaged in an uphill battle against gender inequality, attempting to decrease their double burden. The strength of their numbers and organization as well as the backing of the Rural Workers Association have made it possible for women workers to voice and act upon their demands and concerns. They enjoy the benefits of the revolution's literacy and health campaigns. They no longer must fear that half their children might die while infants, or that they will inevitably lose a conflict with their employer. Through their active participation in the ATC women directly influence the direction and pace of workers' gains, especially those that concern gender issues.

Participation alone, however, provides no guarantee of equality. Hard economic realities narrow the revolution's options. The economy remains based upon women's subordination in low paid jobs. Without more education, technical training, and substantial pressure against traditional sexist attitudes, women at Oscar Turcios will remain concentrated at the bottom of the job hierarchy. And the pressures of the contra war reduce the maneuvering room for women to fight against their oppression.

Notes

1. This phrase is attributed to Gloria Carrión, former AMNLAE leader.
2. Instituto Historico Centroamericano, "The Nicaraguan Family In a Time of Transition," *Envio* 34 (April 1984), p. 2a.

3. Quoted in Randall, *Sandino's Daughters,* p. 14.

4. Patricia Flynn, Aracelly Santana, Helen Shapiro, "Latin American Women: One Myth—Many Realities," *NACLA Report on the Americas* 5 (September-October, 1980), p. 30.

5. See Batya Weinbaum, *The Curious Courtship of Women's Liberation and Socialism* (Boston: South End Press, 1978), and Maria Mies, *Patriarchy and Accumulation on a World Scale.*

6. From AMNLAE "Woman-as-Object to Woman as Revolutionary Force," quoted in Nicaragua Network, *Women in Nicaragua Information Packet* (Washington, D.C.: n.d.), p. 3.

7. Quoted in *Our Socialism* (June/July 1983), p. 13.

8. Interview with Angela Cerda, AMNLAE activist, July 1983.

9. Margaret Randall, *Sandino's Daughters* (Vancouver: New Star Books Ltd., 1981), p. vi.

10. Instituto Historico Centroamericano, "Women in Nicaragua: A Revolution Within a Revolution," *Envio* (July 1983), pp. 1c–9c.

11. Ibid., p. 2c.

12. Tomás Borge, "Women in the Nicaraguan Revolution," in Bruce Marcus, ed., *Nicaragua: The Sandinista People's Revolution* (New York: Pathfinder Press, 1985), pp. 52–53.

13. Deighton et al., *Sweet Ramparts: Women in Revolutionary Nicaragua* (London: War on Want and the Nicaraguan Solidarity Campaign, 1983), p. 65.

14. Instituto Historico, "Women in Nicaragua," p. 2c.

15. *Barricada,* "Nicaragua: una nueva concepción de la mujer," August 16, 1988.

16. CIERA/ATC/CETRA, *Mujer y agroexportación en Nicaragua* (Managua: Centro de Documentación del Instituto Nicaragüense de la Mujer, 1987), pp. 17–18.

17. Comité Ejecutivo Regional, ATC Region I Las Segovias, *Asamblea Regional de Obreras Agricolas,,* p. 3.

18. The following discussion draws from Jane Harris, "Women Farm Workers Meet," *Intercontinental Press* (May 16, 1983), p. 257.

19. ATC, *El Machete* (December 1983), p. 6.

20. Secretaría Nacional de la Mujer, ATC Nacional, *Resoluciones de la Segundo Asamblea Nacional de Obreras Agricolas,* Managua, September 7, 1986.

21. Secretaría Nacional de la Mujer ATC Nacional, *Resoluciones de la III Asamblea Nacional de Obreras Agricolas,* Managua, September 6, 1987.

22. Karl Marx and Frederick Engels, *The German Ideology* (New York: International Publishers, 1987), p. 45.

23. Ibid., p. 67.

24. Ibid., p. 54.

25. Ibid., p. 70.

26. Iris Young, "Beyond the Unhappy Marriage: A Critique of the Dual Systems Theory," in Lydia Sargent, ed., *Women and Revolution: A Discussion of the Unhappy Marriage of Marxism and Feminism* (Boston: South End Press, 1981), p. 51.

27. John Humphrey, "Gender, pay, and skill: manual workers in Brazilian industry," in Haleh Afshar, ed., *Women, Work, and Ideology in the Third World* (London and New York: Tavistock Publications, 1985), pp. 215–216.

28. Lise Vogel, *Marxism and the Oppression of Women* (New Brunswick, New Jersey: Rutgers University Press, 1983), p. 153.

29. Ibid., pp. 153–154.

30. CIERA/ATC/CETRA, *Mujer y agroexportación en Nicaragua* (Managua: Instituto Nicaragüense de la Mujer, 1987), p. 53.

31. Ibid.

32. Ibid.

33. Ibid., p. 55.

34. Ibid.

35. Ibid.

36. Ibid.

37. Ibid.

38. Ibid.

39. Suzanne Lebell, my research assistant, and ATC union local officials gathered the bulk of the survey data.

40. Delphy, *Close to Home*, p. 103.

41. CIERA/ATC/CETRA, *Mujer y agroexportación*, p. 48. This quote shows that the authors of this study accept the distinction between production and reproduction.

42. Interview with Berta Rugama, labor resources technician, August 1988.

43. Oscar Turcios, *Fuerza Laboral Consolidado*, January 1988.

44. This study was based on payroll records of all four production units.

45. This section draws on CIERA/ATC/CETRA, *Mujer y agroexportación*, pp. 56–65.

46. Ibid., p. 61

47. Ibid., p. 64.

48. Interview with Aurora Gonzales, farmworker at Oscar Turcios, July 1987.

49. The following data on tobacco threaders is based on interviews with the 27 women and daily productivity records kept by the norm checker at the Villa Vieja production unit.

50. ATC, *Revolucioón y mujeres del campo* (Managua: Asociación de los Trabajadores del Campo, 1985), p. 36.

51. Ibid., pp. 37–38.

Conclusion

This study has examined class and gender relations on a state enterprise in revolutionary Nicaragua. Both sets of relations are developing as the Sandinista regime strives to transform the public sector's production relations. Although capitalist class relations have been eliminated in Nicaragua's state sector, a new set of class relations are emerging based on the production of surplus labor by workers and the exploitation of organization assets by managers and credential assets by coordinators. Each of the latter two "classes in formation"—managers and coordinators—plays a leading role in the operations of state enterprises. Managers oversee the coordination and integration of a company's division of labor, while coordinators supervise subordinates and provide advice to the controllers of organizational planning and coordination.

Although the Nicaraguan government established a rational wage and salary system in 1983, marked income differentials separate workers, coordinators, and managers in the state sector. On average, managers earn at least four times more than workers and coordinators two to four times more. Thus, while the tremendous pre-revolution disparities in earnings have been eliminated, a hierarchical wage system engenders class conflict on state enterprises. This conflict is characterized by struggles over incentive policies, reclassifications, and the norm system. At the same time, workers attempt to offset part of the impact of uncontrollable inflation by augmenting their incomes through social benefits.

Although class relations in the state sector are riddled by wage battles, the revolution has undermined the authoritarian nature of relations between workers and supervisors. Maltreated as "beasts of burden" under Somoza, rural workers now demand—and receive—the respect of their supervisors. Nevertheless, the elimination of authoritarianism in supervisor-worker relations has led to one unintended, negative consequence: both productivity and quality have declined on state enterprises, eroding the well-being of both workers and supervisors. And while quality-control measures have been introduced on Oscar Turcios and other state farms, it is unclear whether such measures will reap the intended benefits.

The problem of raising productivity and maintaining worker discipline in revolutionary Nicaragua has implications for other movements promoting social change in the Third World. For any social transformation in an economically backward country faces the vast task of reconstruction after the destructive effects of revolutionary war. And the work of reconstruction requires immense austerity and sacrifice from working people. Yet the need for worker disicipline must be matched by fundamental changes in workers' lives. Revolutionary regimes find this dual challenge extremely difficult to meet. The key element in confronting the challenge lies in worker participation. To ensure workers' support for the revolution, they must have a share in the fundamental decisions facing the country; if they are unable to do so, productivity will decline because of the workers' disinterest and resistance, thereby imperiling the revolution itself.

Moreover, revolutionary regimes must recognize that worker participation is the most important aspect of realizing the socialist aspirations of state policies. As the authors of the *Envio* note,

> Technology and whether property is publicly or privately owned is not what defines socialism in its initial stages. In the first phases what counts is the project of building a democratic base where campesinos and workers gain increased power over resources and the freedom to develop them. Without that base, technological development and the creation of a powerful state sector is a risk.[1]

Although workers at Oscar Turcios mainly participate in lower-level economic decision making, the significance of their contribution to management cannot be overstated. Their involvement in determining production priorities, setting norms, and allocating social benefits provides workers with invaluable lessons for their future participation in higher-level decision making. Only a sustained effort to expand and upgrade worker participation throughout Nicaragua's state sector will ensure the consolidation of a self-conscious working class. And only a well-organized, self-conscious working class can prevent the managerial and coordinator groups from converting the revolution into the private domain of a small, skilled elite.

While class relations in Nicaragua's state sector are marked by struggles over living standards and efforts to expand worker participation, gender relations are characterized by the pressure of women workers to overcome patriarchal oppression.Women are transforming gender relations at Oscar Turcios amidst an unprecedented feminization of the rural labor force. Women now comprise a large percentage of the total rural proletariat, work in an increasing number of tasks that once were exclusively held by men, and represent a majority of the permanent labor force in the production of agroexport crops.

Despite the high degree of women's participation in agricultural work, the Rural Workers Association failed to adequately respond to women farmworkers' demands during the revolution's first four years. But in response to strong pressure from the rank and file in 1983, the ATC has worked to increase social benefits for women workers, to strengthen women's participation in training programs, and to challenge the gender-based division of labor on private and state farms. At Oscar Turcios, women now hold 60 percent of the leadership positions in union locals, pressing their demands on a wide array of women's issues.

Nevertheless, women workers on the state enterprise remain concentrated in low-paying manual jobs, subjected to the material and ideological domination of a still powerful patriarchal system. Toiling at home as well as in the workplace, the women on Oscar Turcios face tremendous obstacles in their struggle to organize themselves and fight for improvements. Backed by their sisters in union leadership positions, women workers advance concrete proposals for alleviating the burdens of their double workday. Strengthened by recently-won gains such as canteens at worksites and adult education classes, women workers are now demanding a health care facility, job training courses, and access to birth control.

Women engaged in agricultural labor throughout the Third World can learn three instructive lessons from the experience of Nicaragua's rural women workers. First, to launch an assault against gender oppression, women workers must convert their numerical strength into organizational muscle. Only after mobilizing themselves into a cohesive force did women in the Rural Workers Association take on the sexist practices and ideology of their union federation. Since 1983, hundreds of women have gained union leadership positions, providing an organizational platform for sustained mobilization around women's issues. Second, women workers must develop a theoretical understanding of their oppression, linking an analysis of gender discrimination at the workplace with a critique of sexism in the domestic sphere. At farmworker assemblies throughout the country in 1988, ATC women pressed demands that would lighten their family responsibilities and allow them to devote more time to wage struggles and union participation. Finally, rural women must grasp the importance of creating a national women's organization to fight gender oppression. The fundamental role that the Nicaraguan Women's Association, AMNLAE, plays in the Sandinista revolution has underpinned the social and economic gains of women farmworkers. Although tremendous obstacles continue to block the path to geniune women's emancipation in the countryside, the active presence of a women's organization that counters sexism through policy provides a reservoir of strength for Nicaragua's class-based feminism.

The Sandinista revolution's attempt to transform class and gender relations is multifaceted and laborious. Confronted by war, economic crisis, and the legacy of oppression, Nicaraguan working men and women must devote most of their time and energy to survival tasks. At the same time, the country's state sector employees are demonstrating that painstaking work and democratic participation can lead to significant changes in social structures. Once a genuine peace is won, the opportunity will exist for an even more profound reordering of Nicaraguan society.

Notes

1. Instituto Historico Centroamericano, "The New Economic Package—Will a Popular Model Emerge?" *Envio*, Volume 7 Number 86 (August 1988), p. 48.

Appendix:
Recent Theories on
Class and Gender

The Class Structure of Socialist Societies

Contemporary Marxists have encountered great difficulties in analyzing the emergence of a new class structure in socialist societies. In general terms, two alternative positions can be distinguished. The first holds that a new dominant class, stratum, or elite has established itself in power. Konrad and Szelenyi, for example, argue that "the social structure of early socialism" is a class structure, "and indeed a dichotomous one. . . . At one pole is an evolving class of intellectuals who occupy the position of redistributors, at the other a working class which produces the social surplus but has no right of disposition over it."[1] But they add:

> This dichotomous model of a class structure is not sufficient for purposes of classifying everyone in the society (just as the dichotomy of capitalist and proletarian is not in itself sufficient for purposes of assigning a status to every single person in capitalist society); an ever larger fraction of the population must be assigned to the intermediate strata.[2]

The second approach is best exemplified by Weselowski's analysis of the transformation of the class structure in Poland in which he asserts that there has been a gradual elimination of class differences as a result of the declining importance of the relationship of individuals to the means of production. At the same time, Weselowski sees a diminution in secondary differences related to the nature of work and to attributes of social position such as income, education, and access to cultural goods. Thus, Weselowski denies the emergence of a new dominant class and stresses the eradication of class domination, while recognizing that status differences still exist, as do conflicts of interest between different social groups and strata.[3]

Those Marxists who argue that a new dominant class has emerged in socialist societies differ on how to define precisely the nature of this class. In most cases, their differences center on the new form of economic ownership that the new ruling class exercises in socialist societies.[4] Two of the most interesting positions taken on this issue are held by Donald C. Hodges and Erik Olin Wright. While both these Marxist scholars agree that Marx's class analysis fails to explain class differences under socialism, the two adopt somewhat different stances on how to define the class structure of "actually existing socialism."

Donald C. Hodges and the Bureaucratization of Socialism

Hodges poses the inadequacies of Marx's class analysis for understanding postcapitalist societies in the following manner:

> Because both the capitalists and the landowners are expropriated in postcapitalist societies . . . Marx's structure of classes is unequipped to explain class antagonisms under socialism. Even should the proletariat survive as a class, there will no longer be another class to oppress it. Although functionaries of various kinds enjoy special privileges, Marx's schema includes state functionaries in a classless stratum, and it includes the corresponding functionaries in industry, commerce, and transportation in a higher stratum of the working class. There is simply no basis for future class conflicts within this framework; built into it is the impossibility of class antagonisms in postcapitalist societies. Most Marxists who acknowledge that such antagonisms exist conclude that these societies must still be capitalist. But this conclusion also flies in the face of the facts. Besides denying that class antagonisms can exist in postcapitalist societies, it denies that a social revolution took place in the Soviet Union and Eastern Europe.[5]

Arguing that Marx's model has to be recast for a Marxist understanding of class antagonisms under socialism, Hodges adds a fourth great class to the traditional Marxist trilogy of captitalists, landlords, and workers. This fourth great class is defined by the ownership of "expertise—the specialized administrative, professional, and scientific skills common to functionaries in all walks of life."[6] Hodges asserts that owners of expertise appropriate surplus value in the form of high salaries.

> This is effected through the exploitation of manual workers and the transfer of the surplus they produce into expert hands. Just as high wages help skilled manual workers to recover part of the surplus lost through the exploitation of their labor power by the capitalist, so high salaries enable the intellectual worker to recover the cost of his particular skills along with the entire surplus that might otherwise have accrued to his employer. But that is not all. Unlike the skilled manual worker, he also apppropriates an additonal sum consisting of a portion of the surplus value produced by other workers.[7]

But Hodges' argument does not rest with the assertion of the existence of a fourth great class. He also contends that another class exists in both capitalist and socialist societies. This class comprises "low-qualified workers" who share in the surplus value produced by the working class but who are paid mainly for the labor they perform:

Although they differ from wage earners in pocketing a share of suplus value, they also differ from owners of high-qualified expertise who receive the bulk of their salaries from exploitation. Thus, we may distinguish between a class of major exploiters that receives the bulk of its income from the labor of others and an intermediate or transitional class, a class of petty exploiters that receives the smaller part of its income in this manner.[8]

Thus Hodges recasts Marx's model by making five fundamental claims: (1) expertise is a fourth factor of production; (2) owners of expertise form a fourth great class; (3) owners of expertise appropriate surplus value in the form of high salaries; (4) owners of low-qualified expertise—petty bureaucrats—form an intermediate class between workers and owners of high-qualified expertise; and (5) these petty bureaucrats receive a small part of their income from the labor of others.

Erik Olin Wright and Organization Assets

Wright's recent work on class theory attempts to make *exploitation* the foundation of class analysis so that it can account for the problematic of the "middle class" within capitalism and the historical reality of postcapitalist class structures.[9] Wright derives his restoration of an exploitation-centered concept of class from the writings on exploitation by philosopher John Roemer. Roemer argues that exploitation stems from inequalities in distributions of productive assets, or what is usually called property relations. His argument entails two points. On the one hand, inequalities of assets are sufficient to account for transfers of surplus; on the other hand, different forms of asset inequality define different systems of exploitation. Roemer thus defines classes as positions within the social relations of production derived from these relations of exploitation.

Drawing on Roemer's exploitation-centered concept of class, Wright analyzes exploitation based on what he calls "organization assets":

As both Adam Smith and Marx noted, the technical division of labour among producers was itself a source of productivity. The way the process of production is organized is a productive resource independent of the expenditure of labour power, the use of means of production or the skills of the producer. Of course there is an interrelationship between organization and these other assets, just as there is an interdependence between means of production and skills. But organization—the conditions of coordinated cooperation among producers in a complex division of labour—is a productive resource in its own right.[10]

Wright asserts that in contemporary capitalism, managers control organization assets within specific firms under the guidelines set by the ownership of capital assets by capitalists. Due to the unplanned nature of the capitalist market, no one group of actors controls the technical division of labor across firms. Whereas in capitalism the control over organization assets is limited to the firm, in state bureaucratic socialism the coordination of productive activities extends to the whole society through the central planning organs within the state. By controlling organization assets managers/bureaucrats appropriate and distribute part or all of the socially produced surplus. The class relation involved here is thus between managers/bureaucrats—people who control organization assets—and nonmanagers.[11]

Thus Wright, like Hodges, argues that an exploiting class exists under socialism—the bureaucrats. But whereas Hodges asserts that bureaucrats appropriate the surplus in the form of highs salaries, Wright fails to specify the precise mechanism through which this bureaucratic class extracts surplus labor from workers. At the same time, Wright follows Hodges by pointing to the existence of an intermediate class located between the managers and the workers. He calls the members of this class "experts" who "control their own skills/ knowledge within production, and by virtue of such control are able to appropriate some of the surplus out of production."[12]

Wright thus centers his definition of class on the concept of exploitation and argues that the dominant class in socialist societies is characterized by its ownership of "organization assets." He claims that this class of managers/ bureaucrats appropriates and distributes all or part of the socially produced surplus but neglects to identify the actual process of appropriation. In addition, Wright distinguishes another class of partial exploiters of "skills/credentials," arguing that their ownership rights extend to only a limited part of the social surplus.

Stephen A. Resnick and Richard D. Wolff and the Class Process

Resnick and Wolff argue that Marx's concept of class distinguishes people not according to the "factor of production" or "productive asset" they have or lack, but according to their participation in the production and/or distribution of surplus labor. Marx views class, according to Resnick and Wolff, as one distinct process among the many that constitute social life. The class process is that "in which unpaid surplus-labor is pumped out of direct producers." Resnick and Wolff stress that for Marx class process is one thing, classes are another:

> By classes we understand Marx to mean subdivisions among people according to the particular positions they occupy in the class process, to the precise ways in which they "personify" class processes. People participate in class processes; they thereby occupy class positions. Some people perform necessary and surplus labor— Marx's "direct producers"—while others extract or appropriate surplus labor. This conceptualization of class is complex. First, an individual can and typically does occupy more than one class position and so becomes a member of more than one class. Second, Marx specifies more than the two class positions defined as the performers and extractors of surplus labor.[13]

Resnick and Wolff further note that Marx distinguishes the two class groupings of performers and extractors of surplus labor according to the forms in which the surplus labor is performed. Different forms coexist in varying combinations across human history. Marx uses primitive, communist, slave, feudal, ancient, capitalist, and other distinctions to depict what he calls the "fundamental classes" of history. And Resnick and Wolff emphasize that the fundamentality of these classes consists in their place in Marx's theoretical focus and exposition and not, given the anti-essentialism of Marxian theory, in any notion that they function as "'last instance', final determinants of social change."[14]

Resnick and Wolff assert that the adjective "fundamental" paves the way for positing another sort of class process and thus another set of classes. They call these the "subsumed class process" and the "subsumed classes." Subsumed classes denotes persons occupying a subsumed class position. Such a position occurs within a subsumed class process. The subsumed class process differs from the fundamental class process because it is neither the production nor appropriation of surplus labor or its products. Rather, "the subsumed class process refers to the distribution of already appropriated surplus labor or its products. The subsumed class process entails two positions: distributor and recipient of already appropriated surplus labor or its products."[15]

There are a number of advantages to Resnick and Wolff's reading of Marx. First, by defining class according to people's participation in the production or extraction of surplus labor, they avoid the disputes generated by distinguishing classes in terms of "factor of production" or "productive asset." This does not mean that they regard the ownership or lack of ownership of productive assets as unimportant. Rather, they argue that the process of owning means of production provides "conditions of existence" of class processes.[16] Second, their concept of class is different from the dichotomous theory of traditional Marxism. The notion of subsumed classes allows for the inclusion of other important classes in a social formation, thereby overcoming the tendency in orthodox Marxism of subordinating all other classes in some two-class juxtaposition. Third, by defining class as a process, Resnick and Wolff are able to emphasize the ever-changing aspect of class:

> The Marxian notion of social change or transition refers to a multi-leveled development. All the fundamental and subsumed class processes, as well as all nonclass processes within any social formation, are always changing (given their overdetermined contradictions), are always in transition. Marx makes this point about both class processes in communist as well as in other formations. Existing fundamental and subsumed class processes are not only changing, but some are ceasing to exist while new ones are born.[17]

Fourth, by insisting that class is an adjective, not a noun, Resnick and Wolff avoid identifying human beings by their participation in only one set of social processes:

> Since class is an adjective designating merely two of the many social processes that constitute any human beings or any group of human beings, it is problematic to identify persons or groups by reference to merely two of the many different social processes in which they participate. Without extensive qualification, such identification amounts to essentialist discourse: reducing the complexity of person and group to but one of its many dimensions or determinants. Having argued that Marxian epistemology and Marxian social analysis are pointedly antiessentialist

forms of discourse, it follows that essentialist usages of the term *class* must be rejected in and by Marxian theory.[18]

At the same time, however, certain ambiguities exist in Resnick and Wolff's class analysis in terms of its applicability to an anaysis of state socialist regimes. They make clear in *Knowledge and Class* that in capitalism, "productive capitalists occupy the fundamental capitalist class position of receiver (appropriator) of surplus value."[19]. And elsewhere, in underlining Marx's repeated differentiation between fundamental and subsumed classes, they cite *Theories of Surplus Value:* "[The] capitalist is the person who at first holds the whole surplus-value in his hands no matter how it may be distributed between himself and other people under the names of rent, industrial profit and interest."[20] In post-capitalist social formations, however, there are no capitalists who "receive" or "hold in their hands" the surplus value. Those who appropriate the surplus in state socialism do so in a manner quite distinct from the way capitalists appropriate surplus value in capitalism.

Let us say, for example, that in the Soviet Union, bureaucrats in state ministries and state planning bodies dictate to enterprise directors what to do with the receipts on the sale of products. Does that make them receivers of the surplus or merely distributors of the surplus? And if these bureaucrats are not receivers, who then are the receivers? If Resnick and Wolff claim that the bureaucrats *are* the receivers of the surplus—as well as the subsequent distributors—are they not receivers in a different sense than capitalists? And if, on the other hand, there are no receivers of the surplus product at all in "actually existing socialism," does that mean there is no fundamental class process taking place in these societies? But a careful reading of their work indicates they do believe that a fundamental class process exists in socialist societies. Since Resnick and Wolff do not attempt an analysis of postcapitalist regimes, it is not clear how they would define the two-class grouping of performers and extractors of surplus labor in state socialist societies.

When Resnick and Wolff do briefly treat postcapitalist social formations, they do so cryptically. They speak of the transition to communism in the Soviet Union implying "the presence of noncommunist fundamental class processes" and add: "The capitalist may be prevalent in the social formation while the object of social change is the precise undermining of that prevalence."[21] These titillating passages leave the reader guessing as to where they stand. Is the capitalist fundamental class process really prevalent in the Soviet Union? And if it is, Resnick and Wolff do not explain to the reader why this is so.

This brief overview of recent contributions to a Marxist class analysis of socialist societies demonstrates that substantial differences exist between those Marxists who accept the premise that a new class has consolidated itself in power in socialist societies. While Hodges and Wright agree that the new class rests on a new form of economic ownership, they disagree on the nature of that ownership. And Resnick and Wolff contend that possession of "expertise" or "organization assets" is a *condition of existence* for the fundamental class process in socialist societies, but insist that the production and extraction of surplus labor is the key to the class structure of any social formation, without offering an analysis of postcapitalist social formations.

Gender Relations

Maria Mies, a sociologist and author of several historical works on feminism, made the following observation in 1986:

> For many Third World women, the issue of women's liberation was and is closely connected with the issue of national liberation from colonial and/or neo-colonial dependency, and with the perspective of building up a socialist society. And even many feminists in the West looked at the combination of an anti-imperialist struggle with an anti-patriarchalist struggle with great hope, at least in the early 1970s. As had happened with the students' movement, also large sections of the feminist movement in the West expected the real feminist breakthrough to come from the women's movement in Third World countries which were fighting an anti-imperialist liberation struggle.[22]

Mies points out that today we are faced with "growing evidence of the persistence—or even a renewed introduction—of sexist and patriarchal attitudes and institutions in such countries."[23] A major reason for the persistence of patriarchy in countries conducting national liberation struggles is that they have accepted the widely-believed premise that women's emancipation is a cultural or ideological affair. After the abolition of private property and the socialist transformation of production relations, it is assumed that all remaining problems in the man-woman relation are "cultural lags," ideological survivals of the past "feudal" or "capitalist" society which can be conquered through legal reform, education, persuasion, cultural revolutions and propaganda campaigns. As the man-woman relationship is not regarded as an inherent part of the basic structural relations of production, these measures have had as little success in socialist countries as they had in the capitalist countries. The gap between liberal or socialist ideology embodied in formal laws and constitutions and patriarchal practice is equally wide in both systems.[24]

Arguing against the influence "cultural feminism" has had in the theoretical works of feminists, Mies calls on feminists to be wary of theoretical concepts that lead to idealist and patriarchal positions on women's oppression:

> [I]t is essential that our categories and concepts are such that they help us to transcend capitalist-patriarchy and help us construct a reality in which neither women, men, nor nature are exploited and destroyed. But this presupposes that we understand that women's oppression today is part and parcel of capitalist (or socialist) patriarchal *production relations*, of the paradigm of ever-increasing growth, of ever-increasing forces of production, of unlimited exploitation of nature, of unlimited production of commodities, ever-expanding markets and never-ending accumulation of dead capital. A purely cultural feminist movement will not be able to identify the forces and powers that stand in our way.[25]

To grasp women's oppression as a fundamental aspect of a society's production relations it is necessary to go beyond the analysis of class relations when analyzing the social division of labor. The sexual division of labor—gender inequality—must be taken into account in any analysis of a social formation's production relations.

Theories of Gender Inequality

In her path-breaking book, *Patriarchy at Work,* Sylvia Walby classifies five categories of writings on gender inequality:

> gender inequality as theoretically insignificant or non-existent; gender inequality as derivative from capitalist relations; gender inequality as a result of an autonomous system of patriarchy, which is the primary form of social inequality; gender inequality as resulting from patriarchal relations so intertwined with capitalist relations that they form one system of capitalist patriarchy; gender inequality as the consequence of the interaction of autonomous systems of patriarchy and capitalism (dualist writings).[26]

Since I find the fifth category of writings compelling as well as valuable for an understanding of gender relations in Nicaragua, I will survey some of the most important contributions within that category.

Patriarchy and Capitalism
as Analytically Independent

As Walby observes, the conceptualization of patriarchy as analytically independent yet interacting with capitalism is a major advance on other theories of patriarchy.

> It captures the autonomy of patriarchal relations whilst not ignoring the significance of capitalist relations. It leaves the question of the exact nature of the articulation of the two systems as an open, rather than predetermined, question and provides the essential basis of a theoretical framework for analysing gender inequality.[27]

Writings which view patriarchy and capitalism as analytically independent— "dualist writings"—fall into two general camps: first, those which assign different social spheres to the determination of either patriarchal or capitalist relations; and second, those which view patriarchal and capitalist relations as interconnecting at all levels and spheres of society. Many of the writings in the first group are rather problematic since they allocate patriarchal and capitalist relations to different spheres: those of reproduction and production respectively. The division between material relations into two spheres—reproduction and production—dates back to Engels. In *The Origin of the Family, Private Property and the State,* Engels included in production those activities related to the means of existence, of food, clothing, shelter, and the tools necessary for survival. Reproduction involved the propagation of the species through the reproduction of human beings. Engels further asserted that men were engaged in production, while women were involved in reproduction, and that this division of labor was "natural." Only when production became a more important sphere through its generation of surpluses did women become subordinate to men. These surpluses also comprised the basis of private property, classes, and the state. As private property developed, men confined women to monogamous marriages in order to ensure that their biological sons inherited their property.

The division between reproduction and production should be rejected on many grounds not least of which is the confusion caused by one term being used to represent three different concepts: the reproduction of the entire system of social production, the reproduction of the labor force, and biological or human reproduction. But Walby offers a more telling criticism:

> The distinction between production and reproduction is arbitrary and unsustainable. Almost every task which these writers might allocate to production could in certain circumstances be allocated to reproduction and vice versa. Child-bearing is the only task which could not be randomly allocated. Most of the writings which attempt to make the distinction make an unwarranted biologistic assumption that child care necessarily follows on from childbirth. There is no task currently performed as domestic labour which could not be bought as a service or good on the market; yet typically, when performed in the home it is considered as reproduction, and if outside, production. For instance, food may be purchased at various stages of preparation, right up to the purchase of an entire meal in a restaurant or canteen; cleaning may be bought in the form of a 'servant', 'daily' or contract cleaners; child care may be bought in as child-minders, nurseries or public schools. It is entirely inconsistent to see a person who is paid a wage to do any of these tasks as being engaged in production and a woman who does them unpaid as being engaged in reproduction. They are all work, socially useful and should be seen as production. A distinction between reproduction and production is unfounded and should be rejected in favour of conceptualizing all these tasks as production.[28]

Christine Delphy is one of the few writers who does conceptualize all these tasks as production. I therefore turn to a discussion of her central ideas.

Christine Delphy and the Domestic Mode of Production

Most Marxist feminist analyses have concentrated on the oppression of women in terms of their participation in reproducing labor power within the domestic sphere. That is to say, they see the family as existing in order to sustain indirectly the only form of exploitation recognized under capitalism: that of the workers. For instance, Lise Vogel views domestic labor as the portion of necessary labor performed outside the sphere of capitalist production:

> For the reproduction of labor power to take place, both the domestic and the social components of necessary labor are required. That is, wages may enable a worker to purchase commodities, but additional labor—domestic labor—must generally be performed before they are consumed. In addition. many of the labor processes

associated with the generational replacement of labor power are carried out as part of domestic labor.[29]

However, other feminists influenced by the Marxist tradition have analyzed the family as itself the site of economic exploitation—that of women. Arguing that domestic work and child-rearing are, first, exclusively relegated to women, and, second, unpaid, these feminists conclude that women have a specific relationship to production which is comparable to serfdom. Moreover, they assert that women are exploited in the domestic realm in both capitalist *and* socialist societies. In Christine Delphy's words:

> All contemporary "developed" societies, including "socialist" ones, depend on the unpaid labour of women for domestic services and child-rearing. These services are furnished within the framework of a particular relationship to an individual (the husband). They are excluded from the realm of exchange and consequently have no *value*. They are unpaid. Whatever women receive in return is independent of the work which they perform because it is not handed out in exchange for that work (i.e. as a wage to which their work entitles them), but rather as a gift. The husband's only obligation, which is obviously in his own interest, is to provide for his wife's basic needs, in other words he maintains her labour power.[30]

The main thrust of Delphy's argument is to reject the position that the non-remuneration of domestic work and its exclusion from the domain of economic exchange are due to the very nature of domestic services themselves. Contrary to those who maintain that it is the nature of the work carried out by women that explains their relationship to production, Delphy contends it is women's relations of production that account for the exclusion of their work from the realm of value: "It is women as economic agents who are excluded from the (exchange) market, not what they produce."[31]

Delphy's contribution is to argue not only that housework comprises a form of production as much as work in a factory under capitalist ownership, but to extend that analysis by positing a distinctive mode of production in which that work is performed. Her first premise—that housework is work—is substantiated by showing the basic similarity with tasks which have been definitively assigned to the category of production. For example, she holds that all the processes involved in preparing a loaf of bread for consumption should be considered production:

> When the producer and the consumer are one, as in the farming family, it is obvious that there is a continuum between production and consumption: you sow wheat in order to consume it, you mill it because you cannot consume it in the form of grains, you bake it because you cannot consume it in the form of flour. None of these operations is useful without the others because the goal is the final consumption. It is therefore absurd to introduce a break into the process. This, however, is what happens when only a part of the process is considered productive—up to and including the production of flour—and when the rest of the process, the baking of the bread for example, is condisered non-productive. Either all of the labour involved in making a product which is self-consumed is productive, or none of it is. The

latter hypothesis is absurd because wheat which is eaten could have been sold on the market, in which case it would have had to have been replaced by its equivalent in food purchased on the market.[32]

Delphy contends that women share a common class position in which they are exploited by men as a class: "The appropriation and exploitation of their labour within marriage constitutes the oppression common to all women. Destined as women to become 'the wife of' someone, and thus destined for the same relations of production women constitute but one class."[33] She then argues that not only is women's position within the domestic mode of production the basis of their class exploitation by men, but also that it is their principal form of oppression. Thus she asserts that forms of oppression outside the family stem from women's domestic burden. For example, Delphy views the discrimination that women confront at the workplace as a result of their family obligations.

One of Delphy's most important insights is her claim that a woman's responsibility for raising children should be considered "as a relatively autonomous institution with respect to marriage."[34] She stresses that—whether married or divorced—the responsibility for children's care is borne exclusively by the woman.

> [N]ot only the married and the divorced states but also the state of concubinage, in short all the situations in which children exist and are cared for, have similar characteristics and are different forms of the same insititution, which could be called X. The situation of the unmarried mother can be taken to be its extreme form, and at the same time its most typical form, since the basic dyad is the mother and child. Marriage could be seen as being one of the possible forms of X, in which the basic couple is joined by a man who temporarily participates in the financial upkeep of the child and in return appropriates the woman's labour power.[35]

Delphy goes on to argue that the institution relating to women's exclusive responsibility for child care involves a form of exploitation in addition to the exploitation inherent to the institution of marriage: "This responsibility can be defined as the collective exploitation of women by men, and correlated with this, the collective exemption of men from the cost of reproduction. The individual appropriation of a particular wife's labour by her husband comes over and above this collective appropriation."[36]

Heidi Hartmann and Job Segregation by Sex

Hartmann offers a compelling analysis of gender inequality based on the interrelationship of patriarchy and capitalism. She asserts that most Marxist analyses of women's oppression have concentrated disproportionately on women's relation to capitalism and have largely ignored the independent role of male interest in the oppression of women.

> The woman question has never been the "feminist question." The feminist question is directed at the causes of sexual inequality between women and men, of male dominance over women. Most marxist analyses of women's position take as their question the relationship of women to the economic system, rather than that of

women to men, apparently assuming the latter will be explained in their discussion of the former.[37]

Hartmann argues that patriarchy and capitalism should be viewed as separate structures which have historically had important effects on each other. Although they are analytically independent, they should be recognized as functioning in partnership. She maintains that patriarchy is rooted in men's control over women's labor and builds this into her definition: "We can usefully define patriarchy as a set of social relations between men, which have a material base, and which, though hierarchical, establish or create interdependence and solidarity among men and enable them to dominate women."[38]

Job segregation by sex and the family wage, Hartmann contends, are important forms in which patriarchy and capitalism have interrelated. She argues that men have organized together to exlude women from much paid work mainly, though not only, through the mechanism of job segregation by sex. This device lowers the wages of women in the jobs that remain available to them, and, in turn forces women into remaining dependent on men within the family. Men demand a family wage which perpetuates this situation in which women are deprived of paid work and driven into unpaid domestic work from which men benefit. Hartmann insists that both capital and patriarchy gain from this arrangement.

While I generally agree with Hartmann's analysis, I find her claims about the actual base of patriarchy unclear. The main thesis of her argument is that patriarchy stems from men's control over women's labor: "The material base upon which patriarchy rests lies most fundamentally in men's control over women's labor power."[39] Hartmann focuses on this claim in most of her analysis. But at times her concept of control is so broad as to be rather ambiguous, and she occasionally indicates that other aspects of patriarchy are more fundamental to, and even underlie, this control. For example, she views monogamous heterosexual marriage as a device that allows men to control women's access to resources and their sexuality. This control, in turn, "allows men to control women's labor power, both for the purposes of serving men in many personal and sexual ways and for the purpose of rearing children."[40] Hartmann also points to other social institutions such as "churches, sports, clubs, unions, armies, factories, offices, health centers, the media etc.," as inculcating patriarchal forms of behavior.[41] Consequently, she posits a wide basis for patriarchal relations, thus engendering a rather loose theory: "The material base of patriarchy, then, does not rest solely on childrearing in the family, but on all the social structures that enable men to control women's labor power."[42]

Hartmann's theoretical looseness here contradicts her position in "Capitalism, Patriarchy and Job Segregation by Sex," in which she stresses that job segregation is the foundation for men's control over women's labor. In that essay she insists that male organization, especially in the workplace, which excludes women from most remunerative jobs, is the central basis of patriarchy. Job segregation produces lower wages for women and confines them to inferior positions in the family: "Job segregation by sex, I will argue, is the primary mechanism in capitalist society that maintains the superiority of men over women, because it enforces lower wages for women in the labor market."[43] Thus, on the key question of the basis of patriarchy Hartmann's position is marred by inconsistency and ambiguity.

Nevertheless, Hartmann's work is an innovative and sophisticated attempt to harmonize the analyses by Marxists and feminists without subordinating one to the other. It advances the theory of gender inequality by recognizing patriarchy and capitalism as two separate structures with interracting effects.

Ferguson and Folbre and Sex-Affective Production

While Ferguson and Folbre's analysis of the relationship between patriarchy and capitalism draws heavily on Heidi Hartmann's work, they believe Hartmann overstates the degree of harmony between the two systems:

> Unlike Hartmann . . . we believe that capitalism and patriarchy are wedded in conflict. Their marriage is a truly unhappy one, based upon mutual dependence but weakened by contradictory needs. While capitalist social relations have incorporated many patriarchal forms of domination, they have also weakened some forms of patriarchal control over women. Hartmann and others have failed to appreciate the importance of this contradiction. We attribute this failure to a mistaken tendency to focus exclusively upon women's work in economic production of goods, ignoring what we term sex-affective production: childbearing, childrearing, and the provision of nurturance, affection, and sexual satisfaction.[44]

Ferguson and Folbre argue that Hartmann's failing is symptomatic of much contemporary Marxist and socialist feminist analysis. While socialist feminists have argued for an expansion of the definition of production to include the production of use values within the home (housework or domestic labor), they stick to Marxist orthodoxy by ignoring childbearing, childrearing, and the provision of nurturance, affection, and sexual satisfaction. As Ferguson and Folbre opine:

> Long run changes in the size, composition, and stability of the family, as well as the character of social relations there, inevitably affect the production of labor power. Yet most of the literature concerning domestic labor and value theory ignores these factors. . . . "Reproduction of the laborer" is pictured as the physical reproduction of the adult male. The nature of the labor that wives and mothers perform is seldom explored. Furthermore, the labor time which mothers devote to their children—future workers—is never discussed.[45]

Ferguson and Folbre also note that Marxist feminists who have shown an intrest in family life *per se* dwell on its noneconomic character. As an example they cite Gayle Rubin's essay, "The Traffic in Women," which claims that every society has a sex gender system which organizes and directs sexuality and creates a sex gender identity. Yet Rubin scarcely mentions childbearing and childrearing and treats the sex gender system in terms of expectations, rewards, punishments, and role formation. According to Rubin, the sex gender system organizes the labor process as a whole, but it has no basis in any specific form of production.[46]

Although Ferguson and Folbre concur with much of Rubin's argument, agreeing that the sex gender system affects production as a whole, they argue that it has a special relationship to particular forms of production. As they put their hypothesis:

> *Patriarchal relations and the sex gender system form the social context for specific forms of human (typically, female) labor: labor devoted to bearing and rearing children and nurturing adult men.* In order to emphasize the importance of the labor process itself, we utilize the concept of *sex-affective production.*[47]

Ferguson and Folbre have a special reason for using the concept sex-affective production to describe society's ways of organizing childbearing, childrearing, and the fulfillment of human needs for affection, nurturance, and sexual education. They want to stress that the term *production*—purposeful human behavior which creates use-values—entails far more than the production of tangible goods such as food and clothing. Ferguson and Folbre contend that the bearing and rearing of children, and the provision of affection, nurturance, and sexual satisfaction, all represent use values. "Human labor invested in these tasks," they insist, "cannot be placed lower than other forms of labor in conceptual importance."[48]

Ferguson and Folbre argue that motherhood itself includes not only women's direct responsibilities to children, but also the care and nurturance of adult men. They point to the strong connection between nurturance and affection that mothers provide their offspring and the subordination of their own needs to those of their mate. And they emphasize the oppressive nature of women's role in sex-affective production:

> Although men sometimes engage in sex-affective production, most of its responsibilities and requirements are met by women. This division of labor is not a neutral one, assigning "separate but equal" roles. It is an oppressive one, based upon inequality and reinforced by social relations of domination. Characteristic inequalities include a longer working day with less material and emotional rewards than men, less control over family decisions, and less sexual freedom combined with less sexual satisfaction. Specialization on sex-affective production is also associated with restrictions on options, choices, and remuneration available to women in work outside of the family—restrictions often directly attributed to their presumed or actual mothering role.[49]

I agree with Ferguson and Folbre's depiction of sex-affective production and their claim that any analysis of patriarchy must include an account of the specific forms of labor which women perform.[50] Furthermore, I would argue that an understanding of sex-affective production is also necessary for any effective analysis of worplaces, especially those in which significant numbers of women work. For workplaces are shaped partly by the structural role that the sex-affective production system plays in directing personal choices and options for men and women. Moreover, women's ability to participate in workplace struggles is directly affected by the amount of time and energy they devote to meeting the needs of children and men. In short, analyses of production relations cannot be adequate without taking gender inequality in the home into account.

Notes

1. Quoted in Tom Bottomore, ed., *A Dictionary of Marxist Thought* (Cambridge, Massachusetts: Harvard University Press, 1983), p. 77.

2. Quoted in ibid., p. 77.

3. Ibid.

4. By ownership here I mean effective control, not legal ownership.

5. Donald C. Hodges, *The Bureaucratization of Socialism* (Massachusetts: The University of Massachusetts Press, 1981), p. 16.

6. Ibid., p. 17.

7. Ibid., pp. 13–14.

8. Ibid., p. 46.

9. Erik Olin Wright, "What is Middle about the Middle Class," in John Roemer, ed., *Analytical Marxism* (Cambridge: Cambridge University Press, 1986), pp. 117–118.

10. Ibid., p. 120.

11. Ibid., p. 124.

12. Ibid.

13. Richard D. Wolff and Stephen A. Resnick, *Knowledge and Class: A Marxian Critique of Political Economy* (Chicago and London: The University of Chicago Press, 1987), p. 117.

14. Ibid., p. 118.

15. Ibid.

16. Ibid., p. 143.

17. Ibid., p. 123.

18. Ibid., p. 159.

19. Ibid., p. 143.

20. Quoted in ibid., p. 142.

21. Ibid., p. 124.

22. Maria Mies, *Patriarchy and Accumulation on a World Scale* (London and New Jersey: Zed Books Ltd., 1986), p. 175.

23. Ibid., p. 175.

24. For an interesting discussion of how cultural feminism permeates feminist theory in the socialist countries, see Maxine Molyneaux, "Socialist Countries Old and New: Progress Toward Women Emancipation," *Monthly Review* (July–August 1982), pp. 56–100.

25. Mies, *Patriarchy and Accumulation on a World Scale*, p. 23.

26. Silvia Walby, *Patriarchy at Work* (Minneapolis: University of Minnesota Press, 1986), p. 5.

27. Ibid., p. 33.

28. Ibid., p. 36.

29. Lise Vogel, *Marxism and the Oppression of Women: Toward a Unitary Theory* (New Brunswick, New Jersey: Rutgers University Press, 1983), p. 152.

30. Christine Delphy, *Close to Home: A Materialist Analysis of Women's Oppression* (Amherst: The University of Massachusetts Press, 1984), p. 60.

31. Ibid., p. 60.

32. Ibid., p. 64.

33. Ibid., p. 71.

34. Ibid., p. 124.

35. Ibid., p. 125.

36. Ibid., p. 126.

37. Heidi Hartmann, "The Unhappy Marriage of Marxism and Feminism: Towards a More Progressive Union," in Lydia Sargent, ed., *Women and Revolution: A Discussion of the Unhappy Marriage of Marxism and Feminism* (Boston: South End Press, 1981), pp. 3–4.

38. Ibid., p. 14.

39. Ibid., p. 15.

40. Ibid.

41. Ibid.

42. Ibid., p. 16.

43. Heidi Hartmann, "Capitalism, Patriarchy and Job Segregation by Sex," in Zillah R. Eisenstein, ed., *Capitalist Patriarchy and the Case for Socialist Feminism* (New York: Monthly Review Press, 1979), p. 208.

44. Ann Ferguson and Nancy Folbre, "The Unhappy Marriage of Patriarchy and Capitalism," in Lydia Sargent, ed., *Women and Revolution* (Boston: South End Press, 1981), p. 314.

45. Ibid., pp. 316–317.

46. Ibid., p. 317.

47. Ibid.

48. Ibid., p. 318.

49. Ibid., p. 319.

50. Ibid., p. 318.

Select Bibliography

Afshar, Haleh, ed. *Women, Work, and Ideology in the Third World.* New York: Tavistock Publications, 1985.

Black, George. *Triumph of the People: The Sandinista Revolution in Nicaragua.* London: Zed Press, 1981.

Bolton, Dianne. *Nationalization—A Road to Socialism: The Lessons of Tanzania.* London: Zed Press, 1985.

Booth, John A. *The End and the Begining: The Nicaraguan Revolution.* Boulder, Colorado: Westview Press, 1985.

Bottomore, Tom, ed. *A Dictionary of Marxist Thought.* Cambridge, Massachusetts: Harvard University Press, 1983.

Burawoy, Michael. *The Politics of Production.* London: Verso, 1985.

CEPAL, *Nicaragua: Antecedentes economicos del proceso revolucionario.* CEPAL, 1979.

CIERA/ATC/CETRA, *Mujer y agroexportacion en Nicaragua.* Managua: Instituto Nicaragaüense de la Mujer, 1987.

Colburn, Forrest D. *Post-Revolutionary Nicaragua: State, Class, and the Dilemmas of Agrarian Policy.* Berkeley and Los Angeles, California: University of California Press, 1986.

Collins, Joseph. *What Difference Could a Revolution Make? Food and Farming in the New Nicaragua.* San Francisco: Institute for Food and Development Policy, 1982.

Corrigan, Philip; Ramsay, Harvie; and Sayer, Derek. *Socialist Construction and Marxist Theory: Bolshevism and its Critique.* New York: Monthly Review Press, 1978.

Deighton, Jane; Horsley, Rossana; Stewart, Sarah; and Cain, Cathy. *Sweet Ramparts: Women in Revolutionary Nicaragua.* London: War on Want and the Nicaraguan Solidarity Campaign, 1983.

Delphy, Christine. *Close to Home: A Materialist Analysis of Women's Oppression.* Amherst, Massachusetts: The University of Massachusetts Press, 1984.

Dilling et al. *Nicaragua: A People's Revolution* Washington, D.C.: EPICA Task Force, 1980.

Hodges, Donald C. *The Bureaucratization of Socialism.* Massachusetts: The University of Massachusetts Press, 1981.

Mies, Maria. *Patriarchy and Accumulation on a World Scale: Women in the International Division of Labour.* London and New Jersey: Zed Books Ltd., 1986.

Pateman, Carole. *Participation and Democratic Theory*. New York: Cambridge University Press, 1970.

Randall, Margaret. *Sandino's Daughters*. Vancouver: New Star Books Ltd., 1981.

Resnick, Stephen A., and Wolff, Richard D. *Economics: Marxian versus Neoclassical*. Baltimore, Maryland: The John Hopkins University Press, 1987.

————. *Knowledge and Class: A Marxian Critique of Political Economy*. Chicago: The University of Chicago Press, 1987.

Roemer, John. *Analytical Marxism*. Cambridge: Cambridge University Press, 1986.

Ruchwarger, Gary. *People in Power: Forging a Grassroots Democracy in Nicaragua*. Massachusetts: Bergin & Garvey Publishers, Inc., 1987.

Sargent, Lydia, ed. *Women and Revolution: A Discussion of the Unhappy Marriage of Marxism and Feminism*. Boston, Massachusetts: South End Press, 1981.

Spalding, Rose, J., ed. *The Political Economy of Revolutionary Nicaragua*. Massachusetts: Allen & Unwin, Inc., 1987.

Therbúorn, Goran. *What Does the Ruling Class Do When It Rules?* London: New Left Books, 1978.

Vilas, Carlos M. *The Sandinista Revolution: National Liberation and Social Transformation in Central America*. New York: Monthly Review Press, 1986.

Vogel, Lise. *Marxism and the Oppression of Women: Toward a Unitary Theory*. New Brunswick, New Jersey: Rutgers University Press, 1983.

Walby, Sylvia. *Patriarchy at Work*. Minneapolis, Minnesota: University of Minnesota Press, 1986.

Wheelock, Jaime. *El gran desafío*. Managua: Editorial Nueva Nicaragua, 1983.

Wright, Erik Olin. *Classes*. London: Verso, 1985.

Zimbalist, Andrew. *Case Studies on the Labor Process*. New York: Monthly Review Press, 1979.

Articles, Documents, Reports

AMNLAE. "Woman-as-Object to Woman as Revolutionary Force," in Nicaragua Network, *Women in Nicaragua Information Packet* (Washington, D.C., n.d.), p. 3.

Andrade, Manuel. "Por la Productividad y Eficiencia," *El Machete* 84 (May-June, 1988), p. 15.

Barricada. "Patrones del Cosep no Cumplen," (August 24, 1988), p. 5.

ATC Region I Las Segovias. *Asamblea Regional de Obreras Agricolas*, p. 3.

Austin, James E.; Ickis, John C. "Management, Managers, and Revolution." *World Development* Vol. 14, No. 7 (Great Britain: 1986), pp. 775–790.

Baumeister, Eduardo. "The Structure of Nicaraguan Agriculture and the Sandinista Agrarian Reform," in Richard Harris and Carlos M. Vilas, eds., *Nicaragua: A Revolution Under Siege*. London: Zed Books Ltd., 1985.

Borge, Tomás. "Women in the Nicaraguan Revolution," in Bruce Marcus, ed., *Nicaragua: The Sandinista People's Revolution*. New York: Pathfinder Press, 1985.

Centro de Investigación de la Realidad de América Latina. *"Un Estilo de Trabajo de ATC que da Pautas y Ofrece Logro," Documentos sobre la Mujer* (Managua, October–December 1987), pp. 8–10.

CIERA/ATC/CETRA, *Mujer y agroexportación en Nicaragua* (Managua: Centro de Documentación del Instituto Nicaragüense de la Mujer, 1987), pp. 17–18.

Deere, Carmen Diane et al., "Agrarian Reform and the Transition in Nicaragua: 1979–1983," (unpublished mimeo, November 1983), pp. 5–6.

Deere, Carmen Diane; Marchetti, S.J., Peter. "The Worker-Peasant Alliance in the First Year of the Nicaraguan Agrarian Reform," *Latin American Perspectives* 8 (Spring 1981), p. 53.

Deere, Carmen Diane; Marchetti, S.J., Peter. "The Worker-Peasant Alliance in the First Year of the Nicaraguan Agrarian Reform," *Latin American Perspectives* 29 (Spring 1981), p. 49.

Dellobuono, Richard. "Nicaragua's Emergency Laws: A In-Depth Look." *Nicaraguan Perspectives* 3 (Winter, 1982).

Ehlers, Heliette. *"La organización de los trabajadores, un proceso no acabado," El Machete* 82 (February 1988), p. 11.

Ferguson, Ann, and Folbre, Nancy. "The Unhappy Marriage of Patriarchy and Capitalism," in Lydia Sargent, ed., *Women and Revolution.* Boston: South End Press, 1981

Ferrari, Sergio. *"Nicaragua: Una Nueva Concepción de la Mujer," Barricada,* August 16, 1988, p. 9.

FSLN. *Women and the Sandinista Revolution.* Managua: Editorial Vanguardia, 1987.

Gomez, Eduardo. *Tabaco Nicaragüense.* (Managua: INCAE. 1983)

Gutierrez, Ulises. *Problemas de la Gestión Administrativa de la Empresa Oscar Turcios Chavarria de la Region I Las Segovias.* CIERA MIDINRA, December 1986.

Harris, Jane. "Women Farm Workers Meet," *Intercontinental Press* (May 16, 1983), p. 257.

Harris, Richard. "The Role of Industry in Revolutionary Nicaragua's Mixed Economy," in Richard Harris and Carlos Vilas, eds., *Nicaragua Under Siege.* London: Zed Press, 1985.

Hartmann, Heidi. "Capitalism, Patriarchy and Job Segregation by Sex," in Zillah R. Eisenstein, ed., *Capitalist Patriarchy and the Case for Socialist Feminism.* New York: Monthly Review Press, 1981.

————."The Unhappy Marriage of Marxism and Feminism: Towards a More Progressive Union," in Lydia Sargent, ed., *Women and Revolution: A Discussion of the Unhappy Marriage of Marxism and Feminism.* Boston: South End Press, 1981.

Instituto Historico Centroamericano. "Women in Nicaragua: A Revolution Within a Revolution," *Envio* (July 1983), pp. 1c–9c.

————. "The Nicaraguan Family in a Time of Transition," *Envio* (April 1984), pp. 1c–11c.

————. "Rural Workers Confront the Economic Crisis," *Envio* (May 1987), pp. 24–33.

———. "Economic Reform: Taking it to the Streets," *Envio* (April 1988), pp. 29–30.

———. "Las Medidas de Junio: Paquete Sin Pueblo," *Envio*, (July-August, 1988),

Kaimowitz, David and Thome, Joseph R. "Nicaragua's Agrarian Reform: The First Year," in Thomas T. Walker, ed. *Nicaragua in Revolution.* New York: Praeger, 1982.

Lamphere, Louise. "Fighting the Piece-Rate System: New Dimensions of an Old Struggle in the Apparel Industry," in Andrew Zimbailist, ed., *Case Studies on the Labor Process.* New York: Monthly Review Press, 1979.

MIDINRA. *Plan de Trabajo: Balance y Perspectivas 1988.* Managua: MIDINRA, 1988.

Ministerio de Trabajo. "Resolución del Ministerio de Trabajo Relativa al Pago por Eficiencia en el Desempeno del Cargo," 1986.

Molyneaux, Maxine. "Socialist Countries Old and New: Progress Toward Women's Emancipation," *Monthly Review* (July-August 1982), pp. 56–100.

Montenegro, Sofía. "Unions Must Play a New Role," *Barricada Internacional* (June 2, 1988), pp. 4–5.

Oficina de la Mujer. *Fuerza Laboral Femenina en la Rama Textil-Vestuario Segregación, Salarios y Rotación,* Managua: *Oficina de la Mujer* (May 1987).

Oscar Turcios Chavarria. *Evaluación General: Normas de Trabajo y Salarios,* February 21, 1986.

———. *Recuperación de los Rendimientos y La Jornada Laboral en el Campo,* January 26, 1987, pp. 5–6.

———. *Medidas para la Estabilización de la Fuerza de Trabajo,* August 29, 1987.

———. *Fuerza de Trabajo Problemas Enfrentados y Logros Obtenidos Ciclo 86–87,* September 8, 1987.

———. *Memorandum: Ubicación de Categorias y Salarios,* November 17, 1987.

———. *Evaluación del Desempeno,* 1987.

———. *Convenio de Producción Ciclo 88–89,* March 23, 1988.

———. *Memorandum: Promoción de Escala Salarial,* July 4, 1988.

———. *Informe Evaluativo: Ciclo 87–88, Avance Ciclo 88–89,* July 6, 1988, pp. 4, 7.

———. *Reglamento de Incentivos a traves del Abastecimiento a todos los Trabajadores de la Empresa,* August 15, 1988.

Ruchwarger, Gary. "Children and Cafeterias: Rural Women Organize for Equality," *Nicaraguan Perspectives* 15 (Summer 1988), pp. 16–21, 34.

Secretaria Nacional de la Mujer ATC Nacional, *Resoluciones de la Segundo Asamblea Nacional de Obreras Agricolas,* Managua, September 7, 1986.

———. *Resoluciones de la III Asamblea Nacional de Obreras Agricolas,* Managua, September 6, 1987.

Soto, Orlando Nuñez. "The Third Social Force in National Liberation Movements." *Latin American Perspectives* 29 (Spring 1981), p. 11.

Stahler-Scholk, Richard. *La normación del Trabajo en Nicaragua, 1983–1986.* CRIES, Managua, October 1985.

Young, Iris. "Beyond the Unhappy Marriage: A Critique of the Dual Systems Theory," in Lydia Sargent, ed., *Women and Revolution: A Discussion of the Unhappy Marriage of Marxism and Feminism.* Boston: South End Press, 1981.

Zimmerman, Matilde. "How Sandinistas Won Over the Nicaraguan Farmers," *Intercontinental Press* (April 20, 1981), p. 391.

Interviews

Boniche, Rene, enterprise technician, February 1988.
Castellano, Eligio, SUE member, January 8, 1988.
Cerda, Angela, AMNLAE activist, July 1983.
Enriquez, Magda, manual worker, August 1987.
Gutierrez, Nohelia, kitchen supervisor, July 1988.
Perez, Vivian, SUE general secretary, September 9, 1986.
Martinez, Alberto, ATC secretary of organization, August 10, 1987.
Paz, Marietta, director of human resources, January 1988.
Rugama, Berta, enterprise labor force technician, August 19, 1988.
Salinas, Julian, SUE secretary of production, January 1988.
Talavara, Olga Maria, ATC secretary of production in main processing facility.
Valdivia, Hector, enterprise director, August 17, 1988.

Index